Spiritual Thoughts

By Wes Fessler

BETTER HALF PUBLICATIONS

Layton, Utah

BETTER HALF PUBLICATIONS, OCTOBER 1996

Spiritual Thoughts

Cover and poetry by Wes Fessler

Edited by Stephenie Glissmeyer

Printed by Publisher's Press
Salt Lake City, Utah

ISBN: 0-9655856-0-3

Copyright © 1996 Wes Fessler
All Rights Reserved

This book is dedicated to my wonderful wife Carrie, to my daughter Sierra, and to all who seek after their talents with the help of the Lord.

ACHIEVEMENT

When I'm Gone

Each day in life a tale we write.
Our mark is made in black and white.
Some take control and plan it out,
while others drag their pens with doubt.
But time moves on for everyone,
no matter if we walk or run.
And every day our tale is told.
Some fade away as they grow old.
The key is in the use of time.
Some choose to lean. Some choose to climb.
But in a world where splendor thrives,
how can so many waste their lives?
Content to live the "normal" way,
in idleness they choose to stay.
What happened to their childhood dreams?
Somehow they've disappeared it seems.
But there are some who make their mark,
not blindly walking in the dark.
They know they won't be here for long.
They write their stories clear and strong.
Since every day could be their last,
they see the future, not the past.
We all have stories yet to write.
We can fade out, or shine our light.
All I can say is when I'm gone,
I want my story to live on.

AGING

More Than We See

God has given us day that we may know the night.
He has given us time to do good in His sight.
He has given us seasons of growth and decay,
where a life bears its beauty and whithers away.
Mortal life is our chance to develop and grow,
as we blossom and flourish, our true colors show.
In the autumn our leaves curl and fall to the ground.
And our external beauty no longer is found.
By the winter our stem reunites with the Earth.
It is only a memory of intimate worth.
Though the shell of our physical body is gone,
in our roots there is beauty that always lives on.
When the spring of eternity brings a new day,
all the glory again will shine forth in array.
In the soul we make progress as long as we try,
for a flower is more than we see with the eye.

APPEARANCE

Don't Take Me As I Am

Don't take me as I am, for I am not what I appear.
I'm tender as a lamb, but somehow I ended up here.
A home for wolves and predators to hunt me in the wild.
In this land there's no mercy for the peaceful and the mild.
So I have turned away from tenderness I used to share.
I mask myself with coldness and pretend that I don't care.
Appearing as a threat to anyone who comes my way.
I'm just another wolf now, I scare everyone away.
Survival brings disaster when its course has been denied.
It does not make exceptions, it makes laws all must abide.
To live, I've turned to stone and locked my tender soul within.
Now those who see my callousness can never make it in.
But those who look more closely find much more than at a glance.
They learn that I'm not such a rock if they dare take the chance.
Sometimes I may seem hostile, filling everyone with fear,
but please don't take me as I am; I'm not what I appear.

ATONEMENT

Thoughtless Deeds

As I contemplate my Savior,
how He suffered for my sin,
I feel anguish for my weakness;
My soul bellows from within.
I remember my shortcomings,
my uncaring, thoughtless deeds.
And I can't help but envision
my poor Savior as He bleeds.
Every time I fail and falter
sinking into filthy mud,
with each selfish, prideful action
falls another drop of blood.
I must not add to His anguish.
I must not add to His pain.
I must choose my actions wisely
and from evil thoughts refrain.
Every time I feel temptation
I know I can make it flee,
when I think about the Savior
and the pain he felt for me.

ATTITUDE

All Under Control

I don't believe that we are doomed to failure,
but I feel my best when ready for the worst.
'Cause a life these days is not easy to endure,
when the rich are blessed, and all the poor are cursed.
It might take a while, but we will work it out.
With a mighty hope we'll overcome the doubt.
With our heads held high and eyes upon the goal,
we're going to make it now. It's all under control.
I know I'm not always so optimistic,
and in fact, sometimes I really bring you down.
Still you always help to make my life simplistic.
And with a little time you turn me right around.
It might take a while, but we will work it out.
With a mighty hope we'll overcome the doubt.
With our heads held high and eyes upon the goal,
we're going to make it now. It's all under control.
There still are countless obstacles before us,
and adversity that makes us so confused.
But I know that we will conquer with complete trust.
We'll overcome our fears and face them quite amused.
It might take a while, but we will work it out.
With a mighty hope we'll overcome the doubt;
With our heads held high and eyes upon the goal,
we're going to make it now. It's all under control.

ATTITUDE

Your Own Way

When every will and thrill has gone,
you have to change, or just move on.
You cannot live without your heart.
For what is life, to play a part?
When you don't have a joke to tell,
and all you do is scream and yell,
you need to step aside and see
your life the way it ought to be.
Are things worth getting stressed about,
worth causing you to wail and pout?
Weigh every loss against each gain.
Don't let each day be full of pain.
You have to do what you enjoy,
for in repression there's no joy.
So seek your dreams where they may go,
and when you catch them you will know.
The will and thrill will come again.
You'll find your happiness and then
your heart will be in all you do.
You might just tell a joke or two.
Do what it takes, don't waste away.
Give life your best in your own way.

BAPTISM

The First Leap

In each glorious life a foundation is laid,
where the spirit takes hold, and connection is made.
Where a soul is enlightened with knowledge of God,
as it travels in footsteps the Savior once trod.
When a prayer in the heart yields an echo of peace,
a new purpose in life causes sorrow to cease.
Every day has more meaning, to walk in the light.
There is more motivation to do what is right.
The example of Jesus encompasses thought,
and the puzzle is solved, every piece in its slot.
When the spirit bears witness to truth in the heart,
one can choose to be baptized to make a new start.
In a whole new beginning without any sin,
there is freedom to grow toward heaven within.
A baptism is covenant binding and real;
to obey the commandments however we feel.
To be baptized is taking the first leap toward
our eternal commitment of serving the Lord.

BLESSINGS

Recognizing Blessings

In my life I've had the good and bad that come to everyone,
and sometimes I simply marvel at the things that I have done.
It is not that they're spectacular, or worth bragging about.
It is only strange to me how many good things I've left out.
I remember how I fell that day and how I broke my arm,
but back then I failed to see how God protected me from harm.
I recall the car crash that I had. My fenders were crushed in,
but I didn't think at all of how much worse it could have been.
I remember how I lost my job. It really was unfair.
But I did not see the options that the Lord had placed right there.
I have been so narrow minded that I've only seen the bad.
I just didn't know back then how many blessings I have had.
It's a lesson that I learn each day, that I am given much.
It's recognizing blessings and the Savior's loving touch.
There is so much good in my life now, I finally can see,
that God has always been there, gently watching over me.

CHARITY

How To Give

In the last dispensation, society's way
is to take all you can without giving away.
It is taking advantage of other's bad luck,
for the self-serving purpose of making a buck.
In these times we are tested to see what we'll do,
if we'll wither away, or if we will stand true.
We are sifted and sorted with each step we take.
Will we weather the storm, or will we snap and break?
Can we give of ourselves without thought of reward?
Can we keep in our hearts the pure love of the Lord?
Will we humble ourselves to see others in need,
or will we be too prideful and too full of greed?
We were saved for the last days, demanding great strength
to endure to the end and prove worthy at length.
There are many elect who will falter and fail,
but with charity we can together prevail.
For the truth is eternal, it can't be denied.
We must learn how to give. We must give up our pride.

CHILDREN

Just A Kid

It seems so strange to see your life of childhood in the past,
the times of obscure sorrow and great joy.
The never-ending days of youth reached their conclusion fast,
and I am no more innocent and coy.
My childhood days are summed up with my wife's upon the wall,
together all within one single frame.
And looking up, I reminisce, now able to recall
lost memories that once burned with brilliant flame.
So long ago I did not know what life would be today;
I'm grateful that back then I was so blind.
For if I knew back then about the price I'd have to pay,
I never would have lived with peace of mind.
The rules of life were different then and I could even smile,
for no real reason, I just wanted to.
And even though I bummed around in such a lazy style,
I never had to look for things to do.
It did not really matter where I went or what I did,
my happiness was simply just to live.
And though I did not have a lot when I was just a kid,
I found it so much more easy to give.
I was quite satisfied in giving smiles that returned
that's all it took to make it a great day.
Now looking once again into the mirror, I have learned
that as I've grown, I've turned the other way.
How can it be that growing up can make a life so low,
as hearts with age are transformed into stone?
It seems that we've forgotten something we already know,
that love will fade away unless it's shown.
What beautiful reminders are the pictures of the past,
where you just smiled because you wanted to.
I wish the world would change and live as young again at last,
so every smile could be returned to you.

CHOICES

Lessons Of Life

After thousands of years don't you think man should learn
how to make a wise choice and not take a wrong turn?
There are volumes of books on the library shelf,
but each man learns the lessons of life by himself.
We are warned of the dangers that we should avoid,
but until we explore them, we still feel a void.
So we fall into ditches we knew all about.
And we finally admit there is a better route.
Why does man pay a price he does not have to pay?
Why are we so inclined to do things our own way?
It is part of our nature that makes us unique.
We must live our own way, or we'll always be weak.
But in time we'll be happy with how we have grown.
'Cause the best things in life we must learn on our own.

JESUS CHRIST

Tears In The Rain

He walked the Earth the same as any other man today.
He lived through all the trials found in youth,
but He always held a steady course and never turned astray.
He believed the only way was in the truth.
He lived as man and suffered more than any man could bare.
He felt agony to free us all from pain.
Still so many turn away from Him and just don't seem to care.
I believe His tears are falling in the rain.
He gave everything to show us all how we can choose the right.
He wanted every sheep to find the way.
He loved everyone so dearly, and He found a true delight
in helping any sheep that lost its way.
He lived as man and suffered more than any man could bare.
He felt agony to free us all from pain.
Still so many turn away from Him and just don't seem to care.
I believe His tears are falling in the rain.
At the times when all rejected Him and left Him all alone,
He would pray for them, forgiving every deed.
And when they hung Him on the cross with spikes that pierced His bone,
He died for us still thinking of our need.
He lived as man and suffered more than any man could bare.
He felt agony to free us all from pain.
Still so many turn away from Him and just don't seem to care.
I believe His tears are falling in the rain.
I know that Jesus lives again and watches from on high.
He loves us all more than I can explain.
And maybe if we think of Him, when we look to the sky,
His tears won't have to fall as does the rain.

JESUS CHRIST

That Man Upon The Wall

A friend of mine once asked, "Who is that man upon the wall?"
I answered, "He is Jesus Christ who died to save us all."
He asked me if I knew Him, and with joy I said I did.
For I felt His loving presence standing in the room amid.
He asked me what He meant to me, but I had no reply.
I owed my Savior everything, and for him I would die.
I wanted my dear friend to feel the spirit which was there,
for that would be the only way he'd know how much I care.
I said, "This is our Brother, everyone can know it's true,
and if you pray sincerely you can feel what I feel too."
He prayed that very evening with a sincere, longing heart.
Then the spirit fell upon him, and he saw the heavens part.
He knew the simple truth and felt the glory of it all,
for once again he saw the face that was upon my wall.

CHRISTMAS

The True Meaning Of Christmas

The true meaning of Christmas, has it all been lost
in the dizzying shopping and enormous cost?
Has the Christmas tree covered the face on the wall?
Have the families spent all their time at the mall?
Are the candy canes sweeter than praise to His name?
And is Santa at fault for such glory and fame?
Have the presents more meaning than just giving love?
Is it wrong to have Christmas lights shining above?
If the Savior were here, what do you think He'd say?
Would He tell us it's not right to behave this way?
Or would He see that Christmas is as it should be,
That a star shines for Him at the top of the tree.
That the people are giving like never before.
And instead of forgetting, they're praising Him more.
While so much about Christmas today is so new,
the true meaning of Christmas is all up to you.

CHRISTMAS

A Legend Of Santa

A legend of Santa I heard long ago,
but just where it came from I really don't know.
It started one night with one very bright star
that brought men together, from near and from far.
They came bearing gifts for a newly born king,
without understanding of what it would bring.
Somehow as He grew, He remembered the joy
these giving men gave him when he was a boy.
His life full of giving made everyone see
that giving it all can make all mankind free.
But then when he left, no one knew where he'd gone.
Though nobody sees him, his legend lives on.
The gifts always come on the night of his star,
and everyone feels how enchanting they are.
A happy old man who knows who's good and bad,
to this day gives his all to make everyone glad.
And though no one's certain of just where he lives,
there isn't a soul who denies that he gives.
As "Santa" has shown us its simple and clear,
that we should all give every day of the year.

COMMANDMENTS

Why We Have Commandments

Imagine what the world would be if we did not have rules.
We would not be society. We'd be a bunch of fools.
Like a batch of selfish bullies fighting for a piece of pie,
we could never work together and most likely we'd all die.
We are all diverse by nature and diversity is good,
but if we aren't bound by rules there is no hope for brotherhood.
This is why we have commandments, they are not to hold us back.
God has given us His wisdom to help keep us right on track.
The commandments show God's children though unique as we may be,
that we all have things in common. Things we really need to see.
The commandments give us freedom to unite for good of all.
They help us think of others and allow us to stand tall.
I fear to think what life would be if God did not make rules.
It's hard to build a mansion if you don't have any tools.

COMMITTMENT

Set Into Stone

When a choice is made of value
it should be set into stone,
with a firmness of conviction
and a dedicated tone.
If strong measures are not taken
to stand up for what you choose,
you have already decided
that you're in the game to lose.
For a wandering heart is mindless
following its appetite.
And it ventures into danger
when the wrong appears as right.
It is wise to know your limits
and know when you're in too deep.
But you should not make a promise
that you don't intend to keep.
If you contemplate your journey
and set out upon the track,
make your mind sincere and certain
that you won't be turning back.

COMMUNICATION

Who Will Listen?

There is something to say
for two people today
who can somehow convey what they feel.
For too often we fear
others won't want to hear,
and we both end up with a bad deal.
But there is no reward
when you're stiff as a board
and you can't say what you really think.
When you keep it inside
and your ego's denied,
you may have to go talk to a shrink!
There are people out there
who are rude and don't care,
and you're lucky if they'll just say "hi."
But there are a good few
who will listen to you
and perhaps take the time to reply.
There are plenty of fakes
who won't do what it takes,
and don't hear anything that you say.
But if there's one or two
you can really talk to,
then what else do you need anyway?

COMPASSION

Childlike Eyes

If we viewed one another as children,
could we see past the little mistakes?
If we saw one another as family,
could we bypass the foolish heartaches?
We exist in a world of disorder.
We are strangers from one family.
We are all of us brothers and sisters.
We have more common bonds than we see.
It is easy to understand children.
When they do something wrong, we forgive.
Our compassion for children is boundless.
For a child we have so much to give.
From the mercy we have for our children
we can build a compassion for all.
As we learn to be more understanding
many walls of impatience will fall.
There is nothing that lightens a burden
when a journey is painful to take,
as a person who gives you compassion
and who honestly cares for your sake.
We must try to be more understanding.
We must see through more childlike eyes.
When we see someone down in a struggle,
we should always help them to arise.

CONSCIENCE

Hear The Voice

Every soul who lives today,
in spirit realms chose to obey
the Lord's command to live on Earth,
to grow in knowledge, and in worth.
Where all begin with a clean slate,
a chance to slowly fill a plate
with all the victuals of life,
from happiness, to pain and strife.
A freedom never known before,
a whole new world to go explore.
But all to Heaven it must lead
and all is counted, every deed.
The Lord considered every soul,
that not a one would miss the goal;
if he would listen deep inside
to hear the voice, the spirit guide.
A conscience there to show the way,
to seek the Savior every day;
that we may live with him again,
if we endure unto the end.
But conscience speaks in quiet ways,
and any soul who veers or strays
in ways of sin can never hear.
The spirit's voice will disappear.
For all are free to choose their track,
and conscience can not bring them back,
unless they turn to God once more,
then conscience speaks just as before.
Whenever conscience yields to sin
and spirit is not heard within,
it may be time to recognize
behavior that may not be wise.
For spirit only will commune
with one who keeps his soul in tune;
and if he feels the need to roam
how will he ever make it home?

CONTENTMENT

It's Time For Resolutions

The holidays are over, all except for New Year's Day.
The Christmas lights are coming down and being put away.
The credit cards are all topped off. Where did the money go?
Not even this year's tax returns will pay off what we owe.
It's time for resolutions, not just promises to break.
We never seem to get far on the money that we make.
This year we will do better, we'll put money in the bank.
But we need a new car, I'm tired of driving that old tank.
And then there's our computer, it's already three-years-old.
With what they have out now, it is a dinosaur I'm told.
We have to live within our means, but our means are so small.
We need to buy a home, but we can't even buy one wall.
The money makes me angry, we are always wanting more.
Last year our goal was to be rich, but we're still pretty poor.
This year let's make our goal to be happy with what we've got.
We may not have all that we want, but we do have a lot.
We have each other most of all. That's worth much more to me.
It proves again that in this world the best things come for free.
This year my resolution is to spend more time with you,
and after that, I guess I'll try to save some money too.

CONTENTMENT

The Spending Game

They say money and possessions don't bring happiness and joy,
and there really is a lot of truth to that.
But the spending game afflicts us like an evil schemer's ploy,
still we wonder why our wallets are so flat.
There is glamour in new cars and mansions high upon a hill,
but before you buy, you should give it some thought.
'Cause it may be quite a shock when life has become one big bill,
and you really can't afford the things you've bought.
It is not always low wages or high taxes at the source,
it is often simply, always wanting more.
When we're paid a little more we buy again and it gets worse,
still we never figure out why we're so poor.
I'll admit that it is true, there may be some though very few,
with more money than they'll ever get to spend;
but if this type isn't you, it would be wise to get a clue,
'cause if you don't you will be broke until the end.
If you can be content with everything you have today,
you'll be far ahead of those who play the game.
You will feel much more at ease and even find some time to play,
and you may just have some money to your name.

COURAGE

Learn To Jump

There is always a risk in whatever you do.
It may not seem that way, but it really is true.
There is no guarantee everything will go right.
Even well planned events, sometimes end in a fight.
There are risks that seem great and some risks that seem small,
but you stop at the bottom however you fall.
If you take tiny steps getting into to the pool,
all the others who jumped are now swimming and cool.
When you take any chance it may cause you some pain,
so why not take the risks that can bring the most gain?
If you play, play to win. Give it all that you've got.
Learn to jump in the pool or you're going to be hot.

DATING

The Right One

I am tired of dating,
but I cannot quit.
With each person I date
I don't know what I'll get.
Everything seems so perfect
before the first date.
We can talk. We can laugh.
Everything is just great.
But in time I discover
what they are inside.
There are things that come out
that they once tried to hide.
I am frightened away
by who they really are,
by their lack of respect,
and their ugly old car.
I believe it is true
what they say in the myth.
You can not live without,
and you can not live with.
But I can't give up yet,
for I still have a prayer,
that the person for me
is still somewhere out there.
So I keep going out
and I try to have fun.
I just hope that one day
I will pick the right one.

DEATH

I Will

I will go and do thy bidding.
I will live by thy command.
I will take each footstep willing,
as thou lead me by the hand.
Take me down into the vineyard.
Pass the veil before my eyes.
I will labor Dearest Shepherd.
I will grow to be more wise.
I will learn the temporary.
I will face each tragic end.
But in firmness I won't vary,
I'll remain a loyal friend.
I will love my Earthly family.
I will serve as thou desire.
I will face those who despise me.
I will overcome the ire.
I will do thy bidding only
'till thou takest me away.
Then I'll join thee in thy kingdom
on that great and glorious day.
I will follow thee forever,
though mortality will cease.
In thy labor I will glory
with an everlasting peace.

DETERMINATION

Why Do I Want?

Why do I want what I can't get?
Trying to grow, falling in debt.
All that I've done, little to show.
More that I learn, more I don't know.
My wife and child, counting on me.
Where are the things that come for free?
All of my time, just to get by.
Both of us work. People ask why.
Willing to do what it will take.
Hoping to find my lucky break.
Such great ideas. Why do they fail?
I'm just a dog chasing my tail.
But I'm a fool and I don't quit.
When life throws blows, I just get hit.
Why do I want? It's just my pride.
Maybe I'll lose, but still I tried.

DETERMINATION

I'll Be Free Or I'll Die

Morning train, whistle blows.
Downtown street traffic grows.
Working here. Don't know why.
City life, do or die.
What I want, not around.
Happiness isn't found
where a life can't be free.
Greater things meant to be.
Fighting hard to get out,
to what life's all about,
for the few who defy
common life, getting by.
There is more to be done.
There's a race to be run.
But it takes time to grow,
pushing hard, moving slow.
It is true, it's a game
where the poor stay the same.
And there's only one cure,
living life insecure.
That is why few succeed.
It is painful to bleed.
And the risk still remains,
death may strike in the pains.
There is no guarantee
that the bound can break free,
but I've chosen to try.
I'll be free or I'll die.

DETERMINATION

To The Top

Time is holding me back
from the goals I pursue.
I am moving along,
but my course is untrue.
It has always been clear
where I think I should go.
But the progress I make
is depressingly slow.
I am rowing a boat
on a river upstream.
I am fighting the flow.
Things are not as they seem.
What I sought at the start,
now is not quite the same.
I have had to adjust
and re-focus my aim.
But the point of this fight
is I'm closer today
to achieving my dreams
than I was yesterday.
It may not come with ease.
It may not come with speed.
But with patience and work
I will get what I need.
At the end I will not
say I tried, but I failed.
I will say I pressed on
and I finally prevailed.
For the trials of life
are not far in between.
They flare up in a flash
and are seldom foreseen.
Our success all depends
on our strength to endure.
To hang on through the storm
'till it's safe and secure.
When in life it seems you're
at the end of your rope
climb your way to the top
and don't ever lose hope.

DISCIPLINE

Take The Blame

How we blame youth today
for the criminal way
they behave when they finally get caught.
Though the kids do the deeds,
sometimes we plant the seeds
long before they give wrong any thought.
Are we morally strong?
It has been far too long
since our nation stood for what is right.
Do we have what it takes
to show children what makes
them responsible in the Lord's sight?
Kids are growing up fast,
and in view of the past,
we are not showing them the right way.
We must reach deep inside,
we must do more to guide,
in the things that we do and we say.
Children should take the blame
for their deeds just the same;
they should learn consequence from the start.
But before we can say
they're the ones who should pay,
we must be sure that we've done our part.

ENDURANCE

Get On Your Feet

As we live, we are subject to falls and pain.
From our youth we are challenged to fail or gain.
As when learning to walk, a child falls sometimes,
but a child always gets up again and climbs.
When you're down it may seem that you can't get up,
but there's always a way if you don't give up.
In a world where we're all too afraid to fall,
there is little to learn or achieve at all.
There is more to be learned when we try and fail,
gaining wisdom to fight until we prevail.
We only can lose when we fail to rise;
for the child who will walk, is the one who tries.
Never let any fall keep you down for long.
When you get on your feet you can do no wrong.

FAITH

Grown From A Seed

There would be no looking forward. There would be nothing to see.
If a spark of hope from heaven were not given unto me.
But from youth I knew my duty. It was simple from the start.
There would always come a blessing if the Lord was in my heart.
As a child I learned the value of a friendship with the Lord.
And I found as I was prayerful, I was not ever ignored.
It was faith that brought me this far, it all started with a spark.
It is faith that always saves me when I wander in the dark.
There are times I don't remember what I learned so long ago.
Sometimes life is so confusing, I just don't know where to go.
But I always find a way out, when I try my faith once more.
And my testimony grows in ways it never has before.
The very root of progress is a faith grown from a seed.
A faith that with the Savior, one is able to succeed.

FAMILY

Is It So Wrong ?

Complexity in life is something I don't understand.
You work your fingers to the bone just for a piece of land.
How difficult the modern world has made it just to live,
as money falls from fingertips like water through a sieve.
A great amount of time is spent conforming to the mold,
and ending up a product, that is labeled and controlled.
The energy exerted, yields so little in reward.
When costs exceed the wages, what can anyone afford?
Surviving at the minimum until the day you die,
caught up in the complexity no time to wonder why.
What made the world a puzzle where the pieces all must fit,
or face the consequence of being thrown into a pit?
Is it so wrong to wish that I could live for those I love?
To simply bring them joy, away from all the push and shove?
Why do I face such scorn when I stay home from work or school
to help my stranded mother when her car runs out of fuel?
And why is it so terrible to sit at home and write
my lovely wife a letter that may brighten up her night?
Or what about the children? They are growing up so fast.
Am I to just ignore them until childhood has passed?
I'm sorry if my absence from work made your anger burst,
but you will have to wait your turn, I PUT MY FAMILY FIRST!!

FATHERHOOD

Something You Should Know

I have felt amazing joy since I found out that you are here,
though the evidence that you exist I cannot see or hear.
There are only moods and sicknesses your mother has each day,
and the grand feeling of fatherhood that will not go away.
Still I know that you are with us, and I wish that you could see
all the happiness and vibrance you've already given me.
Every day I reach for higher goals in everything I do.
I am doing all I can to give the very best to you.
I look forward to the days ahead together we will share,
and I hope that when you need me you will always know I'm there.
For a father is a busy man and sometimes too much so,
but I promise I'll make time for you that's something you should know.
I am writing you this letter as a written guarantee.
So one day if I forget these things, just bring it back to me.
I love you my dear child, I'm so glad God blessed me with you.
And I will give all that I can to show you it is true.

FATHERHOOD

The Most Joyous Gift Of All

This Christmas brought a wonderful surprise,
a happiness that we could not disguise.
My wife and I prepared all that we could
to make sure that this Christmas would be good.
We spent too much the way we always do.
We traveled home to see our families too.
It all went very well just as we planned.
We had more fun than we thought we could stand.
Then as our happy holiday neared end,
and we had no more greeting cards to send,
we were given the most joyous gift of all.
It was something very great, but very small.
That night we learned we'd been given a child.
With such good news we danced around and smiled.
The test was positive without a doubt.
We had so much to be happy about.
This Christmas was the best I ever had.
It felt so good to know I was a dad.

FATHERHOOD

The Busy Man Behind The Scenes

Father's Day began back in 1910,
because mothers can't have all of the fun.
A lady named Dodd recognized men,
since they always seemed to be on the run.

Mothers had a day that was recognized,
'cause a mother always seems to be there;
but a father's job was not realized,
and Mrs. Dodd did not think that was fair.

She started up a brand new holiday,
when the father received presents and praise.
By keeping the father at home one day,
this new tradition became a real craze.

Father always works hard doing his best
and it takes up almost all of his time.
If we don't let him know that we're impressed,
it should surely be considered a crime.

Father's Day is to show how much we care
about the busy man behind the scenes.
One of the few times we are able to share,
and let him know how much to us he means.

FOCUS

"Heartwork"

Do you know your heart's desire?
Is it really all you thought?
Take a look deep through the fire
where the brilliant soul is wrought.
There are boundless paths to choose
and new challenges to face.
While you're sorting through the clues,
it is hard to keep your place.
With an ever-changing course,
never knowing what's ahead;
in the quest to find recourse,
sometimes the heart forgets the head.
Plans may change from day to day.
Chaos marks the human breed.
But there is one simple way
to at least get what you need.
When you've run around too long,
and you can't work out what's right;
you may find you're much more strong,
when on your knees you see the light.
Every heart in time will change,
as molded artwork from inside.
"Heartwork" may seem very strange
until the Savior is your guide.
If your heart is in His hands,
your path will surely be more clear,
and you can face what life demands
without a worry or a fear.

FOCUS

Plain And Simple

From a window high above I took a moment on my own,
to gaze upon a city moving by.
Browning leaves blew from the trees toward a destiny unknown,
as a blind man held a sign and gave a sigh.
I could hear the traffic rushing, but I also heard the breeze.
Images of good and bad mixed into one.
I looked up into the ocean sky to put my mind at ease,
but my eyes could find no comfort in the sun.
I peered into the distance where the land stood all alone.
A place untouched by tools or concrete sands.
With plain and simple elements of water, soil, and stone,
it was a great relief from life's demands.
No man made set of rules or expectations to be found.
No need to live on wages much too low.
A place to feel tranquillity, absorbing every sound,
allowing hidden excellence to show.
And so it is with life, though many fail to comprehend,
that simple gifts of God can be the key.
They free us from confusion and allow us to extend,
to work toward our true capacity.
The modern world's complexity leads many souls astray,
ensnaring them with unavailing strings.
Don't search the world or buy a map, the Lord will lead your way;
the miracles are plain and simple things.

FOCUS

Just for You

As the world runs its course, it is easy to lose
any vision of what means the most.
In the struggle to keep up while falling behind,
there is never a moment to coast.
For the trivial matters are placed on the top
of the list of the things to be done;
while the tasks of real value are buried and lost,
as you spend all your time on the run.
When the deadening process of working each day,
is the ultimate focus of life,
it is critically urgent to take a step back to survey
the cause of this great strife.
It takes only a moment away from it all
to remember the abandoned goals,
but if time is not taken to see where you are,
your whole life may end up full of holes.
Though the hours are few and the labor is great
and it seems there's no time left to spare,
there are times when it's better to live in your dreams
than to find yourself caught in life's snare.
For dreams are a challenge, but they can come true.
You must simply believe they are real,
then reach into your visions and into your heart
and express everything that you feel.
There is little to gain in this bustling world
when surviving is all that you do.
Your potential is great, but to see it achieved
you must take time to live just for you.

FORGIVENESS

More Than You Will Ever Know

Regret cannot account for all the time I've been away.
Sorrow can't explain my troubled heart.
Deficient can not clarify the price I've had to pay.
In shambles, not the way I fell apart.
"I miss you," can not nearly tell the loneliness I feel.
"I need you," can't describe my dire lack.
"I live for you," may never prove my love for you is real.
"I love you," may not ever bring you back.
There's really nothing to describe my life apart from you.
The concept is impossible to show.
My thoughts and feelings can not tell the simple thing so true,
I love you more than you will ever know.

FREE AGENCY

Choosing The Right

Why am I here? What do I have to prove?
Am I destined to fail in my every move?
Can I make any change, or am I led by fate?
Am I making a choice, or just taking the bait?
These are questions I ask when things don't go my way,
and I want to give up in my hopeless dismay.
But I know deep inside that actions I choose,
are of my own free will, though sometimes I may lose.
I have chosen the path that I walk on today,
when I chose the Lord's plan and He showed me the way.
I have no one to blame for my weakness and fear.
It is all up to me, what I'll do while I'm here.
So I'll give my best effort to choosing the right,
then I'll run while I can, with the goal in my sight.
Though I commonly err, I will do what it takes
and perhaps if success will outweigh my mistakes,
I will come to the Lord, and He'll say with a smile,
"Well, you figured it out, but it took you a while!"

FRIENDSHIP

A Friend

There is not a greater treasure
of esteem among mankind.
There is not as rare an honor
that a soul will ever find
than a friend without condition,
never yielding when in strain.
One who shares a common vision
both in pleasure and in pain.
There is nothing as uplifting
when life crumbles into dust,
as a friend who shares your feelings
and in whom you place your trust.
Knowing well your word in private
will in privacy remain;
that in future times of worry
you can speak your mind again.
There is strength in such a friendship
one can find no other place,
and a confidence to deal with
any challenge you may face.
There is nothing as relieving
when you have something to say,
as a friend who cares to listen
and to look at things your way.
A friend who thinks no less of you
if what you say seems wrong,
but shares an honest point of view
that might make you more strong.
There is not a greater blessing
than to have a loyal friend,
who in spite of confrontation
will stand by you to the end.
There is nothing of more value
than to have a friend so true.
It is my most precious honor
having such a friend as you.

GOALS

A Goal

A goal is something positive until it is tried out.
For when we try to prove ourselves, we take an unknown route.
A goal is much more easy when it's said than when it's done.
It takes a lot of patience, and it is not always fun.
A goal is soon abandoned when it seems too hard to do.
But when it's carried to the end, it's great to see it through.
A goal is opportunity for progress and success;
a time to give our very best and never any less.
A goal is contribution to the welfare of a soul;
a way to turn potential into glory as a whole.
A goal is our perfection at long range as we endure.
And every goal we keep makes each new step we take secure.
A goal is something positive for those who do not quit;
for anything worthwhile takes endurance, faith, and wit.

GOALS

Are You Happy Where You Are?

Are you getting what you want?
Are you happy where you are?
Is the road you travel on
going to take you very far?
Do you think there's something more?
Do you feel like getting out?
Can it be this same routine
is what your life is all about?
There is something you can do.
There is something you can try.
You will never get ahead
if you just watch the world go by.
It is easier to say.
It is much harder to do.
But you'll find your goals in life
depend entirely on you.
Do the things that you enjoy.
Do the things that you do best.
When you like the work you do,
you're that much closer to the crest.
Seek your dreams with all your might.
There is no end to the reward.
For happy people are the ones
who don't have time for being bored.

GOD

If Only

If only they knew that I live
and watch them from above.
Would my dear children change their lives
and show a little love?
If only they believed in me
that I provide a way,
would all my children come to me
or turn the other way?
If only I could make them see
the path that brings them back,
would they come running home to me
or would they jump the track?
If only I could carry them,
I would not let them fall;
but I must stand and watch them
hoping they will heed the call.
If only they could know my love.
If only they could see.
Would my dear beloved children
choose to come back home to me?

GRATITUDE

The Work That You Do

I am seldom at home long enough to observe
all the work that you do every day.
But with all that you do, it would take some real nerve
to pretend while I work, you just play.
Now and then when I'm home, finding time to unwind,
I see things I could not see before.
You clean up all the messes I leave behind,
like the shoes I throw out on the floor.
And the dishes I leave to clean up later on,
are not there when I finally come back.
I'm so thankful for you when I find where they've gone,
they are clean on the shelf in a stack.
And the bed that I left such a terrible mess,
with the covers and sheets in a ball,
now is perfectly made and I have to confess,
I feel like I've done nothing at all.
I'm not always aware of the work that you do,
and I know there's a lot I don't see.
But I want you to know I appreciate you
and the many things you do for me.

GRATITUDE

What I Really Want To Say

I have to tell you now
the things I could not tell you then.
I have to let you know
before I lose my chance again.
You mean so much to me,
but I can never show you how.
I wish that I could give you
all my gratitude somehow.
You always cared for me,
though I was not always so good.
And when I said "I can't,"
you always showed me that I could.
You never quit on me
though I would quit all on my own.
You stood there by my side
when I thought I was all alone.
You showed me there was hope
and in the positive a way.
You taught me to be strong
in case you had to be away.
But now that you are gone
I feel I need to learn much more.
How can I give to you
all that you gave to me before?
I owe you everything,
a debt I never can repay.
I love you, I guess that
is what I really want to say.

HAPPINESS

They Might Have Joy

If men are that they might have joy, perhaps we need to change.
For many seeking righteous lives, ideas are very strange.
Some feel they're only living right when serious and straight,
But in this quest they miss the point and come across irate.
Our sins are very serious, that's absolutely true.
But some believe there's something wrong in everything they do!
Still others like to be the judge and point out people's flaws.
They don't take blame for anything, when really they're the cause.
If men are to have happiness, why do they make life sad?
Life should not be such misery, it's really not that bad.
It's always a more pleasant world when people look for good.
It brings a joyful attitude to do the things we should.
No need to look for negative. You find it anywhere.
The point is to seek happiness because it is so rare.

HAPPINESS

You Need Some Fun

Like a snake on a footpath on a hot summer day,
life can jump out and bite you in a most vicious way.
You can struggle and suffer, doing everything right,
but you better beware of the thief in the night.
For a life is not meant for all work and no play,
and the priceless possessions may dwindle away.
It is wise to place effort in the work that you do,
but with all of the stresses you need some fun too.
There is much more to living than making ends meet;
and the bravest of Generals know when to retreat.
So when life tries your patience do what needs to be done,
then forget all that garbage and go have some fun.

HEAVEN

Purpose In Heaven

Do you know why you want to reach heaven?
Do you know what you'll find when you're there?
Do you think of your purpose in heaven?
Do you think you'll just sit in a chair?
Do you seek heaven's door to retire?
Do you think there your journey is through?
Do you think that's the end of the story,
and there won't be a thing left to do?
Take a moment to think of the freeway,
as if it were the way to the Lord.
If you stood there in rush hour traffic,
don't you think you would be pretty bored?
Is it heaven to be in a car jam?
No it's more like the place down below?
When you're stuck and it's bumper to bumper,
it is heaven to even go slow.
Heaven is not the end of the freeway,
but the traffic is much better there.
If you are not afraid of progression,
you can fly like the wind, if you dare.
So prepare now to labor in heaven.
There will always be things to be done.
No, you cannot be lazy in heaven,
but the work there will be much more fun.

HOLIDAYS (THANKSGIVING)

The More Happy Side Of Life

Every year is filled with challenges
that oft bring men to tears,
bogged down by strange relationships
and monetary fears.

As the blows of life keep pounding
every soul into the ground,
it is hard to see the blessings
and the goodness all around.

But if men stand tall, not quitting
in the madness and the strife,
a simple smile can bring out
the more happy side of life.

Though the trials will keep coming
and their days will never cease,
it's just the way we deal with them
that brings sadness or peace.

When life is dealing challenges,
pick up the cards and play,
and with the proper attitude
everything will be O.K.

When counting all the blessings,
throwing all the bad away,
you'll have something to thank God for
and a great Thanksgiving Day.

HOLIDAYS (LABOR DAY)

The Alarm Was To Blame

The rush of working people can be seen on every street,
from the rich in big white limos, to the poor who use their feet.
At first dawn's light the clock alarm starts screaming in my ear,
and instantly my mind decides to try to get in gear.
But not a chance, my hand's already found the snoozing bar.
I'll sleep for ten more minutes, then I'll jump into the car.
My eyes have finally opened and I'm twenty minutes late.
No way I cannot call in sick, the boss will be irate!
But if I'm not at work on time, he'll hate me just the same!
He won't believe me when I tell him the alarm was to blame!
I'm going to lose my job and how am I to pay the bills!
Oh I've got an awful headache, where on Earth are those darned pills!
"Honey, honey? Please wake up. Everything will be O.K.
It seems that you've forgotten that today is Labor Day!"

HOLIDAYS (NEW YEAR'S DAY)

The New Year Will Be Better

Throughout the ages, folks have always praised the New Year's Day,
and hoped that along with it, a good change would come their way.
A time for resolutions and for making simple goals,
to fill the vacancies of life and all the empty holes.
A year can bring most anything, from greatest joy to pain.
The goals are soon forgotten in some corner of the brain.
When life becomes so twisted, why not blame it on a year,
then gather up the ill feelings and place them in the rear.
Why not, the Romans did it with Janus the two faced god,
one face up front and one in back, he must have looked quite odd.
They say the back one looked at all the bad times in the past,
and told the guy in front, "They're catching up, run away fast!"
It's not the wisest thing to put the problems in the back,
they soon enough gang up on you, preparing for attack.
It's better to write down some goals and put them where they're seen.
Only persistent work can really keep life's records clean.
One needs to be reminded, if the goal's to be achieved,
'cause no one likes to work if no reward will be recieved.
By setting realistic goals to place upon the wall,
there's really hope for success and avoidance of a fall.
On New Year's Day face up to problems, don't put them behind,
the new year will be better and you'll have some peace of mind.

HOLIDAYS (EASTER)

When The Easter Bunny Comes

The Easter Bunny comes each year with colored eggs to hide,
but no one ever sees him, although everyone has tried.
He hops along each Easter day to bring the children joy,
and lots of yummy candy that the kids can all enjoy.
The bunny hides the prizes and they're pretty hard to find,
and when the children look for them, it seems that they are blind.
But soon they find the treasures they were searching for so long,
While eating all the candy, it seems nothing can go wrong.
The Easter Bunny hero never fails to make things right,
with too much joy on Easter day for kids to fuss and fight.
The Bunny knows a secret about how this day began,
through perfect love and kindness of the very greatest man.
This special man was Jesus, and He lived quite long ago.
He loved all children dearly and He showed them how to grow.
Whenever children came to Him, He never turned away.
He always had a gift for them and tender things to say.
Jesus was our Savior and He showed us what to do,
to live at peace with everyone in life and make it through.
With love of God and all mankind, He taught us all the way,
to have a life that's filled with love and live with Him someday.
The day He died, the world wept and everyone was sad;
but in three days He lived again, and every soul was glad.
Before He left for heaven He told everyone again,
to make some time for children every day unto the end.
The Easter Bunny listened and he knew he had to share,
A special gift that he could make for children everywhere.
He leaves surprises early, and nobody sees him come,
in hopes that children will believe that Jesus was the one.
When Easter's just a day that only colored eggs are found,
Remember our dear Savior's love and spread it all around.
For Easter is a special day for children to enjoy,
A special gift from Jesus for every girl and boy.

HONESTY

If Everyone Were Honest

If everyone were honest,
we could stop wasting our time.
We could learn to trust each other,
and we'd see the end of crime.
If everyone were honest
and somebody's car broke down,
we would not have a problem
giving them a ride to town.
If everyone were honest,
we could leave for weeks or more,
and we wouldn't have to panic,
'cause we didn't lock the door.
If everyone were honest
and a beggar asked for cash,
we would know he really needs it,
and we'd help him in a flash.
If everyone were honest,
there would be nothing to hide,
and we could all speak freely,
without keeping things inside.
If everyone were honest,
life would truly be the best.
If everyone were honest,
even God would be impressed.

HUMOR

People Who Frown

What is the matter with people who frown?
Why do they always face life looking down?
Why don't they smile at jokes they are told?
Where is their humor? What makes them so cold?
Maybe I'm strange and I should be more sad.
Maybe I'm wrong and life's terribly bad.
Maybe there's something that I didn't see.
Maybe the whole world is out to get me.
Yes, there are problems. We all have our share.
Yes, there are times when we pull out our hair.
We all have problems with sorrow and strife,
but what can you do if you can't laugh at life?
Humor is crucial. It carries you through.
It helps you be happy. It helps you be you.
If you're a frowner, try out a new style.
It may hurt your face, but you really should smile.

HUMILITY

Treasures Of The Road

Somewhere along a journey, a man headed the wrong way;
and though it was all new to him, he thought he'd be O.K.
But this path was the Devil's road. He set it up himself,
to draw this man away from God by giving him some wealth.
The man filled up his pockets with the treasures of the road,
and carried home a heavy and most valuable load.
He bought himself a new car that not many could afford,
and when the people stared at him, he soon forgot the Lord.
He praised that car and always kept it sparkling and clean,
but soon it lost its splendor, which was something unforeseen.
So on he went and bought a very large and spacious home.
It cost a pretty penny and had lots of room to roam.
The people came from miles around to see his newest prize,
and everyone was impressed with its cost and massive size.
The man was proud of this estate and all that it was worth,
and for a while he thought he had the greatest thing on earth.
Somehow the dazzling mansion soon looked plain to this rich man.
And all the treasures he possessed did not seem quite so grand.
In worldly wealth he had the greatest things money could buy,
but he still was not satisfied and wanted to know why.
He left behind the things he owned and went back up the track,
to find real joy and happiness were there when he went back.
He found the road the Lord had made and followed it with care,
And he was never doubtful as he sought the Lord in prayer.
At last he found the happiness that would not go away,
the greatest things in life are free, it's not how much you pay.
The man learned that the Savior's way is not the path of price.
Without the worldly worries he found life is much more nice.

INTEGRITY

I Am Not Afraid

They can take away my living.
They can take away my home.
They can take away my money.
They can leave me out to roam.
But they cannot make me worry,
and they cannot make me sad.
With the spirit I am happy,
and life doesn't seem so bad.
If the world becomes your idle,
then the world becomes your life.
And the world is a gamble
that can cause you major strife.
I am not afraid of failure.
I am not afraid to lose.
I am not afraid of freedom.
I am not afraid to choose.
With the Lord I feel assurance.
Nothing is too hard to do.
I have peace in righteous living,
for I know the gospel's true.
If I had no faith in heaven,
I would fall apart inside.
It makes every bit of difference
when the Lord is on your side.

JEALOUSY

The Envy Of Man

There are reasons for covenants, guidelines, and rules.
The Lord gives them to us and they're valuable tools.
We are taught not to covet with unrighteous greed,
    but to seek after things that we honestly need.
    But at times we all fall in the pit of desire,
and we push others down as we try to move higher.
    Aspiration is good and essential to growth,
    but its worth is defined by its value to both.
    When a mutual gain is the prize of the goal,
    it is working together to strengthen the whole.
When a goal is sought only for selfish advance,
    it consumes any progress that had any chance.
    When there's jealousy no-one is able to win,
    for no-one can progress in the labor of sin.
    If we seek anything, we must seek it for all,
or the envy of man will be man's great downfall.

KINDNESS

To Lift Each Other

Is it possible to build a dream by tearing others down?
Is there any way to fly if we refuse to leave the ground?
Not a gain was ever made while shoving someone else aside.
In the course of stopping others, our momentum is denied.
When we find the good in others, praising them for who they are,
we build speed for one another. We're both able to go far.
It is possible to reach our dreams together if we try.
We must learn to lift each other, if we ever hope to fly.

KINDNESS

Kindness

A poor stray cat who had no home,
was left out on the street to roam.
And no one ever seemed to care
how cold the poor cat was out there.
Sometimes he found nothing to eat.
Not even fish, or thrown out meat.
The cat was grumpy anyway.
He never smiled or liked to play.
He always slept out on the ground.
Perhaps that's why he always frowned.
But then one day he found a friend,
who showed him kindness to the end.
He gave him food and kept him warm,
and made sure he was safe from harm.
No longer was he cold and scared.
He found someone who really cared.
And soon he became kind, not wild.
He often purred and always smiled.
A little kindness means a lot
to those that kindness haven't got.

KNOWLEDGE

What You Don't Know

"What you don't know won't hurt you."
Have you ever heard that phrase?
Whoever made that statement
really had one of those days.
What you don't know will hurt you!
That is what he should have said.
It's hard to find success these days,
unless you use your head.
A solid education
is unequaled in it's worth.
You take your knowledge with you
when you finish life on Earth.
So why not fill your lantern
that with wisdom it may burn?
What you don't know will hurt you
if you don't take time to learn.

LEADERSHIP

A Good Leader

What makes a good leader?
How is one unique?
A good leader's movement
is full of mystique.
In front of the masses.
Surrounding the foe.
A good leader knows
where he's needed to go.
Proactive in nature,
yet willing to wait.
A good leader knows
when to reel in the bait.
A word when essential,
but zealous to hear.
A good leader studies
with listening ear.
A confident manner
with humble regard.
A good leader ready
to sweat and work hard.
Assigning no order
that cannot be done.
A good leader helping
'till triumph is won.
To be a good leader
one must learn to extend,
giving service to others,
as a trustworthy friend.

LIFE

Seasons

In the seasons of life there are glory and gloom,
from the vibrance of spring, to the pale winter's doom.
Every wind has a hope. Every storm has a tear.
Every sunset brings calm and a moment of cheer.
There are warm days and cold. There is sunshine and rain.
Every day has a tone of sweet joy or deep pain.
In the seasons of life the Lord helps us along.
Through the good and the bad we are made to stand strong.

LIFE

What Is It That Matters?

What is it that matters out of every loud claim?
For time flies and shatters those who have no aim.
Life is not long enough to have useless concern
over trivial stuff that can make feelings burn.
For the small things confuse men and lead them astray.
They blindingly use souls to turn them away.
If your life is just spent without making a mark,
no one knows where you went when you've died in the dark.
There is always a way from a source high above,
if you spend every day in sharing Christlike love.
Giving all you posses to make other lives bright,
when it's love you express, you can find your own light.
For the cares everywhere aren't as great as they say.
There is more you can share when you find time to pray.
Many small things combined, crush you like a great tide.
They're determined to grind you down with selfish pride.
But what matters the most is that you are a friend,
that you don't have to boast, and you're willing to bend.
What's important is not letting things get you down.
It's taking what you've got without wearing a frown.
'Cause before you know it your whole life will be through
So be happy and show it in everything that you do.
With the Savior to lead you'll know just what is right.
You'll have all that you need, and be filled with delight.
What it is that matters, when it's all said and done;
is that you tried your best, lived with joy, and had fun!

LIFE

That Great And Glorious Day

How wondrous and amazing are the turning points of life,
when miracles come pouring in eradicating strife.
How humbling and glorious are the trials we must face,
when holding on through heartache, lifts us to a higher place.
How beautiful and gracious are the lessons that we learn,
when following the Savior, eager for Him to return.
What joy befalls a life that has not known its path before,
that finally finds the iron rod and needs to search no more.
What happiness is carried by the soul who loves to give,
that charity to others makes it easier to live.
What eternal peace is given to the couple seeking love,
that finally finds each other with a blessing from above.
How wondrous and amazing is each day upon this earth.
How humbling and glorious to see a child's birth.
How beautiful and gracious is the Savior's love for all.
What joy we find when we in tune can hear his gentle call.
What happiness we feel as we progress along the way.
What eternal peace awaits us at that great and glorious day.

LOVE

I Have Everything

Many times I've been told that love cannot be sold,
but I wonder if rich men agree.
I have seen women cling, with a flash of a ring,
to the ugliest men with money.
There are some who will say that a strong build today
will bring romance that never will die.
But in grunting and strain, with all brawn and no brain,
men are left all alone wondering why.
Still some others have said that by using your head,
you can charm your way into the heart.
But those who always show everything that they know,
are soon told they are not very smart.
It is so very odd that I don't have a wad
to buy love the way so many do.
I am not very smart and my body's not art,
but I have everything, I have you.

LOVE

Something To Enjoy

If a writer needs a tragedy to sell a tale today,
I could never find my story next to you.
I'd be wasting my time searching, but I'd find nothing to say.
As a writer my career would soon be through.
So I'll have to take a different view and tell the tale of joy.
All the happy things will have to fill the page.
But a little optimism might be something to enjoy,
with other stories, full of misery and rage.
You're the balance of my day when stress and pressure bring me down.
You catch my fall and lift my spirit with good cheer.
Being with you always helps me get my feet back on the ground.
You make the madness and confusion disappear.
You're my driving inspiration, urging me to carry on,
even when I feel I've done all I can do.
When I need to push my limits, but my energy is gone,
I can always count on you to pull me through.
There is never need to argue. You support me all the way,
though there are times when you rightly disagree.
You express your honest feelings, putting pride and fear away,
and my eyes open to things I need to see.
You are everything I need. I absolutely can't complain,
and I don't care if the story will not sell.
Though so many want to hear me talk of tragedy and pain,
I will tell them you and I are doing well.

LOVE

You And I

Can you take this? Can you make this bitter tragedy,
something better, that will let a real hope live for me?
Nothing going, nothing knowing, what am I to do?
All I try, to fall and die, no way to see it through.
Walking backwards, can't retract words when all's said and done.
Never learning, falling, burning, looking for someone.
There you were, it seemed so sure, no horror of the past.
A guiding light, availing bright, to count upon at last.
Into the deep, we took the leap, into the great abyss
of tearing claws and deadly jaws, that rarely ever miss.
Our blood was drawn, as we went on, the pains grew sharp and sore.
But at your side, the raging tide, was nothing like before.
At last we found, the solid ground. Securely we stood tall.
On diamond sands, we filled our hands then rose above it all.
Would not believe. Could not conceive, ever long ago,
that life could be so good for me, but with you it is so.
Never slowing, always growing, we are climbing high.
Moving forward, every reward waits for you and I.

LOVE

Out Of The Darkness

Out of the darkness, I finally found
a beautiful world with joy all around.
New hope and good fortune in glorious light,
a change of fate ended the long gloomy night.
Appearances filled with each brilliant ray
that the sun once restricted from coming my way.
Existence transformed with a wondrous glow,
into shimmering spirit to flower and grow.
I looked into heaven to search for the source
of the all mighty power that altered my course.
In a vision the mystery was easy to see,
It was part of a plan. It was all meant to be.
We were tested to see if we'd live as we should,
in a challenge to sort out the bad and the good.
For some time we were left in the dark all alone,
and we had to prove worthy, though all on our own.
We both made mistakes and we frequently fell,
but with all that we went through, we came out quite well.
Then the dreariness vanished, when in came the light.
In that moment we knew we had done something right.
For we found one another as darkness gave way,
and nothing compared to the joy of the day.
Every troublesome worry vanished in the shade,
while our love for each other was brightly displayed.
For out of the darkness, I finally found
a beautiful world, with joy all around.

LOVE

All Along It Was True

Here we are still the same,
same old place, same old game.
Nothing's new, nothing's changed,
still it seems very strange.
All along it was true,
every path led to you.
Though some lured me to stray,
nothing turned me away.
For I knew deep inside,
there was no need to hide.
And I never before
felt so strong, or knew more.
I'd have someone to trust
when my world turned to dust.
And as time drifted by,
there was no question why;
we gave all that we had,
through the good and the bad.
Always finding a way
to grow closer each day.
With the give and the take
we did not have to brake.
And our love was so strong
when we threw out the wrong.
Finding true harmony,
it was all meant to be.
Here we are still the same,
same old place, same old game.
Nothing's changed, nothing's new,
I have always loved you.

LOVE

It Sure Must Be A Miracle

My past was only part of me that never was complete;
I staggered in the darkness tripping over my own feet.
Somehow my mind believed that it knew just where it should go,
but many phony people turned it wildly to and fro.
I grasped at plants that had no roots and could not get a grip,
then filthy mud dripped on my feet and nearly made me slip.
From early on I knew that there was always hope on high,
and sometimes it would be so close, I thought that I could fly.
This was the motivating force which always pulled me through,
and in my darkest hours always it would tell me what to do.
Although I wanted everything to fall into my hands,
I learned that there is work to do in keeping God's commands.
The gospel grew inside of me, though I was far from pure.
I started to stand firmly and it taught me to endure.
When people came into my life and left without a trace,
it used to leave me empty and not knowing my own place.
But when I weighed these fleeing souls against my lasting peace,
it cured me of my ailing heart and caused my pain to cease.
Though there were many in my life who I wanted to stay,
the Lord has taught me much through them and has another way.
Life isn't always what you want, but often what you need,
when you can put away your pride and any selfish greed.
Our Savior works with miracles most bounteous and great;
and he's a good example that good comes to those who wait.
As patience is a virtue and progression is a must,
our lives require faithfulness and quite a lot of trust.
So much I do not understand. I still have far to go,
but lately I've been humbled and there's one thing that I know.
I surely have done something right for I've been greatly blessed;
I'm not sure what the trial was, or how I passed the test.
It sure must be a miracle, it's more than I could do;
the Lord somehow has seen it right to bless my life with you.
There's nothing else that I could ask to bring me more delight;
My prayers have all been answered and it's never felt so right.
Now I have guided footsteps and a pathway that is clear;
I know when we're together that there is no need to fear.
As we walk into the future, everything will be just fine,
for I know the Lord is with us, and I'm grateful that you're mine.

MARRIAGE

Stronger With Age

It has often been said that it dwindles away,
as time passes among any pair.
Isolating each other and turning astray,
leaving nothing in common to share.
Many echoing, sorrowful hearts give advice,
warning those who find love of a fate
that brings torture to souls with a terrible price
that can turn happiness into hate.
I have heard every horror of marriage and found
that each story was brimming with dread.
And the unhappy couples I saw all around
convinced me that I should not be wed.
Then you captured my heart and destroyed every fear;
I forgot everything I was told.
As time passed we grew closer and it became clear,
we should promise to have and to hold.
Everything has been wonderful every day,
I'm so happy that you are my wife.
It is hard to imagine why so many say
that marriage brings sorrow to life.
As the time hurries by, you can see with one look
that our love's getting stronger with age.
Every moment we share, like a wonderful book,
brings excitement with every page.
Now each time I hear stories of love that has died
and relationships ready to end,
I feel so very blessed with my beautiful bride,
my eternal companion and friend.

MARRIAGE

It's Perfect Now With You

The first sound of the morning, sends me running in the dark,
to shower and race to work on time, so that the boss won't bark.
The tasks of morning hours seem so trivial to me,
but somehow I get caught in them from six o'clock 'till three.
Then rushing to the car to make it just in time for school;
if somebody were watching me, they'd take me for a fool.
The night hours spent dozing off, right up on the front row,
my squinted eyes make certain that my grades will end up low.
A cold drink and an aspirin gets me home with reddened eyes,
to homework due the next day, what a wonderful surprise!
Halfway into the reading my head falls into the books,
and I notice how inviting, warm, and cozy the bed looks.
Collapsing to the mattress, as my day is finally through;
as restless as the day has been, it's perfect now with you.

MARRIAGE

To Share Eternity

In an awesome glorious wonder, over challenges and miles,
heaven filled two searching souls with loving hearts and joyful smiles.
As they finally found each other, every piece fell into place,
and the emptiness they once had felt, had gone without a trace.
Time drifted by and they became the dearest, closest friends
with gratitude to powers on high they'd never let it end.
The loving, deep devotion which they felt was meant to be
in everlasting covenant to share eternity.

MARRIAGE

My Eternal Friend

Every step I've taken until now has left me all alone;
and I've learned to just make do with what I've got.
Every crooked path has wounded me and cut me to the bone,
because I never seem to learn from what I'm taught.
In my quest for independence, I was able to survive,
though I had to rush and struggle all the way.
But I found out it takes so much more to really be alive,
than a solitary life of disarray.
Still the loneliness grew stronger, as I searched for something real;
Things just never seemed to turn out as they should.
Then you came along and gave me what I never thought I'd feel,
and my life has really never been so good.
You are everything I needed. You're the shining light of day.
You have cleared all of the darkness from my life.
I'm so glad the Lord has blessed me to be with you every day;
my eternal friend, my sweetheart, and my wife.

MARRIAGE

Eternity With You

I have often clung to feelings that kept me from moving on,
tied to others who were slipping, no foundation to stand on.
Though I tried to justify it, they were dragging me down too.
So to keep from sinking under, I reached out for something new.
The surroundings seemed quite different, but the facts remained the same.
Though it hurt for me to see it, it was just another game.
My whole life was so uncertain, yet I carried on this way
and in time I grew accustomed to each painful parting day.
In my soul I felt a comfort that assured and let me know
that I had a heavenly purpose, and these things would help me grow.
Though it wasn't ever easy to put friendships in the past,
I knew deep within that I must look for something that would last.
The ending of relationships always made me sad before,
but over time I learned from them, and the wounds weren't quite so sore.
When at times my mind would wander, wanting love and finding doubt,
the Lord always gave me comfort, and I knew it would work out.
In every passing love, I learned what I should and should not do,
so in future times perhaps the disagreements would be few.
I became a better person, or at least it seemed that way,
and the people who I went out with seemed more inclined to stay.
As I thought of others more and worried less for my concerns,
I found what I gave was little, when compared with the returns.
Then at last it really happened, we were finally prepared,
heaven brought us both together into something rarely shared.
The lessons learned from others made our pathway smooth and straight
In good and bad we compromise, and things work out just great.
You are everything I've hoped for, you are truly my best friend,
and each day I pray that our love will not ever have to end.
I love you for forever, and forever I'll be true.
It is such a joy for me to share eternity with you.

MISSIONARY WORK

Good News

How fortunate I feel when I turn on the evening news.
It always helps me see that I have everything to lose.
I have a testimony of the Savior that is strong.
I know that when I follow Him, He never leads me wrong.
I have a sense of conscience and the spirit on my side.
I know what is important and it's not the TV guide.
How sad it is to see the news, for many do not know.
It's hard to watch God's children, when they don't know where to go.
With all that I've been given, I have more than what I need.
It isn't hard to see, the Lord has many sheep to feed.
The gospel is a blessing everybody should enjoy.
By bringing souls to Christ, one finds a treasure chest of joy.
If we all share the gospel, it's impossible to lose.
And maybe when the TV's on we'll finally have good news.

MORALITY

Never Follow The Crowd

Does it matter if people are moral today?
For the most part, man's virtue is passing away,
making room for acceptance of scheme and deceit
with a new breed of man, "the immoral elite,"
who have no set of rules or beliefs to go by.
They just say, "If it feels good, let's give it a try."
But the law of the Lord is still firmly intact,
and it can not be swayed by a man's wrongful act.
No majority vote can deny God's command.
All mankind can revolt, but the truth will still stand.
The Lord clearly defined what is wrong and what's right.
We all know what it takes to do good in His sight.
To be moral is greatly important today.
To have peace in your heart there is no other way.
You must stand on your own and be morally strong.
Never follow the crowd, what they're doing is wrong.

MOTIVATION

Ability

There is nothing to stop you
from making a gain,
though the world has its madness,
its sorrows, and pain.
You alone can determine
the path you will choose,
and nobody can tell you
that you have to lose.
All the tools that you need
to excel, you possess.
And by using them wisely,
you bring out your best.
When you open your eyes,
it is easy to find
all the things you could not see,
when you were so blind.
Then with patience and poise,
as you strive for the goal;
you'll excel like a champ,
finding joy in your soul.
All the progress you want
comes by not looking back,
and by keeping your focus
ahead one the track.
You will stride with the mighty,
and quickly achieve
everything that you hope for
and truly believe.

MOTHERHOOD

The Best A Mom Can Be

As this day has been approaching, I've reflected on the past.
The way you were my dearest friend and how we always had a blast.
The way the family got together with a party just for you,
but how you wouldn't eat your cake 'till everybody else was through.
It wasn't only on your birthday, it was really all the time.
Sometimes you even gave me money while you didn't have a dime.
I didn't always recognize it, but you always cared for me.
You sacrificed so many things to make sure I would be happy.
If there is any love in my heart, it is all because of you.
With selflessness and charity, you always pull me through.
I don't believe that I can repay all you've done for me,
but I must say I love you. You're the best a mom can be.

MOTHERHOOD

It's Great To Be Your Son

Oh how I wish I could repay all you have done for me.
The way you sheltered me from harm, but still let me run free,
to live and learn the ways of life, with values you hold dear.
The way you shared my youthful years with gentleness and cheer.
My debt is great for your concern about the way I grew.
You understood my heart, and when I needed help you knew.
I never had to worry when I needed your support.
You gave me all I needed and I never came out short.
You went without the things you need so I'd have what I like.
You went without new clothes so I could have that brand new bike.
It was that way with everything, you always thought of me,
and gave your all to help me be the man that I should be.
Oh how I wish I could repay the many things you've done.
Dear mother, I love you so much. It's great to be your son.

OBEDIENCE

One Great Test

Is it better to obey?
Is it worth the price I'll pay?
If it's only this one time,
is it really such a crime?
What's the difference if I do?
Everybody else does too.
What's the big deal anyway?
Who cares if I act this way?
These are questions that arise
when a person is not wise.
When temptation clouds the seen
and the judgment is not keen.
There's one question, one great test.
Asking this, one knows what's best.
"If He stood here in my shoes,
is this what the Lord would choose?"

OPTIMISM

What Is Right

A problem is a question with no answer to be found,
a struggle that destroys each leap with falling to the ground.

A challenge is a trial of our faith in who we are,
a chance to surmount fear and reach a greater world afar.

Depression is a carcass slowly turning into dust,
left to the mercy of the wind and torn with every gust.

Ambition is a steadfast course toward a worthy goal,
an ever driven passion to perfect a growing soul.

Confusion is disorder, like a bombshell's aftermath,
a stomach wrenching torment in a realm of dreaded wrath.

Conviction is a treasure map where every mark is clear,
a source of guided wisdom moving forward without fear.

A failure is a dire lack of seeing what is right,
a grim and gloomy outlook, never looking to the light.

Success is when the negative is seen and understood,
yet one can keep his focus dwelling mostly on the good.

PARENTHOOD

Easy To Say

Time has run out.
I did not reach the goal.
A new father to be.
How can I fit the role?
I don't have a good job,
and she has to work too.
In a matter of months
the whole plan fell right through.
It was easy to say
just a short time ago,
"You'll be home with the child,
and I'll pay all we owe."
So we left it at that
and went on just the same,
but now time has run out,
and there's no one to blame.
There is no pot of gold
waiting for me to find.
There is no place to hide
in the back of my mind.
There is only a treasure
of much greater worth
that is soon to arrive
in miraculous birth.
Though it never seemed real,
as it does to us now,
we will do all we can,
and we'll make it somehow.
We are sure to lose sleep
and perhaps even hair!
But this gift from above
is beyond all compare.

PARENTHOOD

Beyond Any Compare

It was the greatest miracle, as she was born that day.
Emotion welled within our hearts, for she was here to stay.
The sight of her was beautiful beyond any compare.
And tears of joy were falling, as we finally held her there.
She gave our lives new meaning. A new reason to achieve.
She made the unbelievable so easy to believe.
How sweet it is to know the Lord is watching over me.
How sweet it is to be a part of this great family.

PARENTHOOD

Aint This The Life

Aint this the life; the way it should be?
My mom and my dad are such suckers for me.
It is so fun. I know them so well.
I know they'll come running, if I start to yell.
I may be small, but I'm pretty smart.
While mom grabs the milk, I put toys in the cart.
My life is good. My future looks bright.
I keep mom and dad up with me every night.
What can I say? When you're cute as me,
you just lie around and relax by the sea.

PATRIOTISM

America

America
is in my heart.
America
I love.
America
a wondrous place.
America
above.
America
the beautiful.
America
the great.
America
the brotherhood.
America
the hate.
America
religion and
America
for God.
America
a precious land,
America
to trod.
America
the freedom and
America
the law.
America
to others is
America
of awe.
America
a proving ground.
America
to grow.

America
in happiness.
America
in woe.
America
conservative.
America
extreme.
America
a future and
America
a dream.
America
the glorious.
America
to see.
America
the only place.
America
for me.

PEACE

Like A Child

Sunny day! First this spring.
Want to do anything
but stay home, locked inside.
Want to go for a ride.
Studying for a test.
But right now I need rest.
I can't think while the sun
calls me out, "Come have fun!"
Books are thrown. Pages fly!
Grab the keys. Don't ask why.
On the road. What a day,
for a clean get away.
No more stress on my mind.
Feels so good to unwind.
It is such a reward.
I feel close to the Lord.
Simple things mean so much.
It's not hard to lose touch
with the Lord's simple truth,
that we all knew in youth.
As we grow, we lose sight,
when our time gets more tight.
We forget why we're here
when we run in high gear.
Life demands us to give
all we have just to live.
We must do what it takes.
But sometimes we need breaks
to get back our lost strength,
and be stronger at length.
Having minds clear and true,
with the gospel in view,
we can face life again
like a child, but as men.

PRAYER

It All Starts With A Prayer

What is right? What is wrong?
What is there in being strong?
What am I going to do?
What on earth is really true?
What is good? What is bad?
What success have I had?
What am I working for?
I am always wanting more.
How can I find content
with the way my life is spent?
Worthy goals, what are they?
Goals are changing every day.
Reaching one. Moving on.
Seems like nothings getting done.
Does it lead anywhere?
Is there something all can share?
One right way, we should go.
Something everyone can know.
We are not all the same.
We all have a different aim.
What I do, you do not.
We all vary quite a lot.
But we can find the way.
It is not so far away.
Everyone on their own
must reach into the unknown.
With the world put aside,
if we put away our pride,
everyone can find out
what life here is all about.
For a prayer to the Lord
cannot ever be ignored.
And when prayer is sincere,
everything is crystal clear.
There's a plan. There's a way.
There's a great and glorious day.
It is right. It is good.
It can all be understood.
It is just. It is fair.
It all starts with a prayer.

PRE-EXISTENCE

Freedom Is Power

At the very beginning, before life on Earth,
we were born unto God in a spiritual birth.
And our family was great, both in beauty and size,
but we soon reached our limit of growing more wise.
So two brothers stood forth, each came up with a plan
that would bring greater knowledge and glory to man.
The Lord offered men freedom to choose wrong or right.
They must all make it back by their courage and might.
But then Satan said, "I won't let anyone choose!
I will force them all back, so nobody will lose."
With progression in mind, God said, "Let them be free.
If they do not return, it was not meant to be."
And then Satan rebelled, saying, "Just follow me!
You will have all you want and you'll have it for free."
So a third of our family went with him instead.
And God cast Satan out with all those he misled.
But the rest of us chose to follow the Lord's plan,
and we make the best choices we possibly can.
As we live now on Earth, knowing what we went through,
we can all make it back. We can all remain true.
For our freedom is power to prove in God's sight
that we're true to the faith and we'll do what is right.

PRIDE

Is It Evil?

Is it evil to be evil?
Well before you nod your head,
think about the implications.
There is more in what was said.
Is it wrong to make an error?
Is it bad to slip and fall?
Is it terrible to play the game,
but somehow drop the ball?
We are all in this together.
We are all children of God.
We all struggle in the journey
to hold to the iron rod.
Some of us may not seem perfect,
some may even lose the way,
but how is the person greater,
who does nothing as they stray.
Is it evil to be evil?
What is best and what is worst?
Before we blame somebody else,
we ought to look at ourselves first.

PROCRASTINATION

Time To Snooze

Time is not a resource you can lay on a shelf,
if you want to get anything done.
When you finally return to pick up where you left,
you may search for the time and find none.
As the deadlines arrive while you're lying in bed,
you may find you're too restless to sleep.
And the longer you lie there, the more tension grows
'cause you know that you're in way too deep.
At this point in the darkness you must make a choice,
either get up or lie there in bed.
Either way, you are not going to get any sleep
with the chaos that's now in your head.
To keep up with the world in a race with no end,
there is never a moment to lose;
but please take my advice, don't let time pass you by,
or like me, you won't have time to snooze.

PROCRASTINATION

Worst Things First

Sometimes we put off doing things that we don't want to do.
We hope that they will get done by somebody passing through.
Or we may just ignore them, hoping they will go away.
We try to win the game when we're ahead, with our delay.
Sometimes this method works, the problem gets solved by itself.
But most problems get worse if we just place them on a shelf.
Our health is an example of something we can't let go.
If we don't take care of ourselves, it won't take long to show.
At least we'll smell like dirty socks, at worst we just might die.
Still many let their health decline, while idly standing by.
The same applies to many things we've put aside and cursed,
but we are so much better off when we do *worst things first*.
For when the worst part's over, we can do what we enjoy,
'cause we've already done the things that bother and annoy.
And now the time is ours to use in any way we please.
We get much more accomplished when our minds are put at ease.
So if procrastination is the part that you've rehearsed,
you'll feel a whole lot better if you do the *worst things first*.

PROFANITY

Is Anyone Offended?

I marvel at the words I hear
in passing commonly.
It seems with every sentence
there's an adjective set free.
The conversation's interesting,
aside from all of that,
but with the foul description
I forget where we were at.
Profanity is everywhere,
it's even on TV.
Is anyone offended?
Well, perhaps it's only me.
I see no use for junk mail,
or a phone without a chord.
Why can't we all communicate,
like we do with the Lord?
Pretend that He is listening,
for he really is in fact.
He knows what we are saying,
and He knows the way we act.
Profanity is ugliness,
however you appear.
If you want to talk ugly,
please just do not do it here.

PROGRESSION

Deserving Of Praise

Nothing is easy deserving of praise.
Much is required to get by these days.
Much more is needed to really succeed.
More than you have, maybe more than you need.
If we're all equal, as some say we are,
why do some fail while some others go far?
If there is freedom and justice for all,
why are the poor always taking the fall?
Where are the laws that make everything fair?
Once elected, politicians don't care.
Where are the values they all care about?
The world has grown selfish and left others out.
How can you gain in a world without rules,
turned down, rejected, and taken for fools?
The answer is not in the stock market crash,
not even in real estate, houses, or cash.
It lies in a quiet place not many know.
It follows a plan that allows us to grow.
The answer is deep in the realm of the heart,
where worldly matters don't have any part.
Where success is measured by how hard you try,
and not by your status or how much you buy.
Your trek back to heaven, you take at your pace,
and with the Lord's help it all falls into place.
Progression is simple, although it's a test.
We're only required to give it our best.
No, nothing comes easy deserving of praise.
We need to work hard without any delays.
Don't look to the world if you want to succeed.
With faith in the Lord, you have all that you need.

PROGRESSION

The Climb

At the base of the mountain, God's children begin a parlous climb,
a decision each made long before, to live on earth for time.
Arriving in a strange world, without memory of the past,
then when placed before a mountain, children can be quite aghast.
But the way to go is clear, when casting eyes toward the sky,
as heavenly hands reach out to all, enticing them to try.
When the simple souls of children trust the Lord with all their might,
they begin their journey upward with their footsteps sure and light.
It does not take long, though before they take a look back down,
discovering they no longer are secure upon the ground.
A child of God feels heavy when faced with challenges of life;
the mountain base is hazardous with potential of great strife.
Steep cliffs wall out the young who climb and try to instill fright,
with rocky sharp edged blades which threaten everyone with plight.
Loose rocks lie on the slopes, in multitudes of falling shale
that grab at climbing feet and drag them down to no avail.
Weeds and briars, full of thorns, are hazards one must face;
they prick and stab at anyone who cannot find his place.
A child of God must choose his every move with greatest care,
for Satan's traps are deadly and can be found everywhere.
Still in the dread of falling, there is comfort, peace, and bliss;
the Lord is always there to help when things have gone amiss.
And parents stand above on a much smoother slope above,
who help and guide their children with great tenderness and love.
But every child of God must find their own way to the top,
and they alone determine whether they will climb or drop.
While parents stretch their hands out to their children who may fall;
the climbing child must decide if he will heed the call.
Any soul who takes the challenge to progress and overcome,
finds it easier to climb when shaking off the cumbersome.
Looking steadfast to the goal and settling for nothing less,
then mapping out the smartest way and giving it the test.
For climbing is a challenge, but it's something all can learn,
and when the Lord is kept in mind, the blessings all return.
Then on again the climber moves into a different stage,
when youth has reached its sunset, as life turns another page.
This portion of the mountain climb looks unconstrained and sure,
but other trials exist here which the climber must endure.
Experience brings knowledge and conviction to achieve,
still one must know his Source Of Strength and constantly believe.

PROGRESSION

Frequently, its when the way seems easily surmounted
that men slip up, because the little trials have been discounted.
When all that matters most is overshadowed with neglect,
it's no surprising thing to find your whole life end up wrecked.
There are so many things to keep in order every day,
but nothing is impossible, the Lord provides a way.
And families can grow together, happily and strong,
together helping each to climb, with spirit and with song.
For nothing thwarts the Devil like a family that is one.
A close eternal family keeps him always on the run.
For keeping things in order is a vital mortal task
and if there is any question, we just need to kneel and ask.
The answers are all there for us when we know what to do.
Achieving dreams is possible, because the Gospel's true.
Then moving on with confidence, we reach the final stage,
that faces every soul as they reach a more advanced age.
The Lord made this path smooth, so tired limbs can reach the peak
by dropping off life's past regrets, becoming more humble and meek.
This is the time to look back at all that's been said and done
and come to peace with God and earth, to know the battle's won.
Nearing the top with a dear spouse, with still so much ahead,
now knowing with contentment for eternity they've wed.
And finally from the top the climbers see what they've achieved;
there is beauty all around and still much more to be received.
Everything endured upon the climb was worth the gorgeous sight
of doing all the Lord has asked, to then receive His light.
And when the climbers find the joy of progress to the top,
they're sure to be more pleased again to know they will not stop.
For progress is eternal and there is much more to achieve;
and the Lord gives joy to everyone who always will believe.

PROGRESSION

A Mission To Fulfill

Every life that knows the gospel, has a mission to fulfill.
Every step along the journey, takes a lot of faith and will.
There are trials we alone can bear that no one else can take.
There are times we need to do our part for someone else's sake.
It is easy to lose sight of all that really needs to be.
The pressures of our daily lives can make it difficult to see.
But there's a path for all to follow, and it doesn't go away.
It only takes our faith and courage, to keep on the narrow way.
There is not any need for money, or possessions, on the Earth;
for what you build yourself in heaven is the real measure of worth.
The mission of our lives will tell us what we're able to afford;
if we we will live our lives for luxury, or humbly seek the Lord.
For where our treasures are, we're sure to find our hearts somewhere nearby,
and if we fail to seek the Lord, our hearts are worthless when we die.
In all we do, we must remember that our Savior leads the way,
and when we place our faith in Him, our treasures never go away.
The greatest gift we have to offer is to serve our fellow men,
in this we serve our Savior too, and we can live with Him again.

PROPHETS

A Truly Great Man

God has followed a pattern of speaking to man,
from the day He made Adam a part of the plan.
He has chosen His prophets to teach us the way
to return to His presence in Heaven someday.
Through the prophets we learn how to improve our lives,
to prepare for the day when our judgment arrives.
Every prophet of God has a big job to do.
They must teach us what's right and record scripture too.
Just imagine if you were a prophet today
and your job was to keep man from slipping away.
With the way the world is, do you think you'd succeed?
Could you get the whole world to face up to their need?
Everyone has their freedom to act as they choose.
Even prophets can't keep us from choosing to lose.
They may not save us all, but for those who they can,
any prophet of God is a truly great man.

RELATIONSHIPS

Memories Never Made

Why is it that I never notice until it's too late?
When you ask for my attention, and I say you'll have to wait.
I get so caught up in other things I don't care much about.
While I spend my time achieving, somehow you end up left out.
I tell you this is just the way it has to be right now,
and I can only give you what my schedule will allow.
But since I'm working hard, one day we'll have more time to share,
and then I'll have more time for you, to show you that I care.
Still that's no consolation for your loneliness right now.
You'd rather have attention than my hopeful distant vow.
Your tears revealed the truth, though you tried not to let it show.
I wish I'd seen it sooner, but again I was too slow.
So many plans I've made for you, only to be delayed.
How can I say I'm sorry for the memories never made?

RELATIONSHIPS

When I'm A Fool

There are times when I'm a fool,
forgetting what I should do
to show my love for you in every way.
When the tension builds inside,
there is no reason to hide,
but somehow I end up lost along the way.
Then I look into your eyes
and the trouble all subsides.
All that matters, once again is crystal clear.
When I search within my mind
it is wonderful to find
you're the answer, all I need is you right here.

RELATIONSHIPS

Something Like The Wind

Sunday came and two began a life in a new place.
The separate lives they once had lived, vanished without a trace.
The concept of eternity still seemed like fantasy.
Togetherness, the here and now, and still so much to see.
When entering the chapel, it came clear as summer sky,
that feeling deep inside them would remain as years went by.
It wasn't always obvious, just something like the wind;
but if you stopped to notice it, you'd feel it pouring in.
The silent calm assurance of forever, two as one
was the driving force of unity, with glory of the sun.
Still the comfort, ever present, sometimes seems so far away,
for love requires effort and attention every day.
The couple learned that happiness is all within control,
by putting one another first and giving heart and soul.
The key is in the feeling, it can unlock any door,
and by heeding its direction there is happiness and more.
Whenever problems great or small come threatening to destroy,
they stop to hear the spirit's voice and share eternal joy.
For nothing can destroy the bonds of everlasting love,
when walking hand in hand with guided footsteps from above.

RELATIONSHIPS

Foolish Cares

Many times the world reaches out to pull me deep inside,
and it seems that I forget about the angel by my side.
When all foolish cares surround me, pressure builds inside my head,
and sometimes when I should turn to you, I turn away instead.
But believe me there is more to it than what you see outside,
and if you were not there for me, by now I may have died.
When I'm burdened with too much to bear and nothing turns out right,
I end up amid confusion, it is not a pretty sight.
But please understand that when I'm down and life seems so unfair,
it is such a comfort to me, just to know that you are there.
When you're with me it does not take long for all the smoke to clear,
any troubles that were on my mind instantly disappear.
Nothing matters any more than you, you're everything to me.
Whether lost or found, with you is where I always want to be.

RELATIONSHIPS

A Foolish Dream

Many lives have crossed the path of mine,
to pause, to rest, or read a sign.
The road is rough and full of snares
that frighten anyone who cares.
But for a while a closeness grows.
I give my love. It truly shows.
Then joy returns to me as well,
and life's not just an empty shell.
For just a while it seems to me
that there's a place for me to be.
In loving arms to have, to hold,
the story is so often told.
But time builds walls that I can't see,
and doubt builds up inside of me.
The distance grows within my mind,
and love once strong is left behind.
So once again I'm on my own.
I have to walk the road alone.
What is this trap I have inside?
Can it be only selfish pride,
or is there something more ahead?
Am I just simply being led
with flowering love along the way
that brings me joy, but cannot stay?
Until I find someone I need
to share a love that's free of greed.
Who'll walk with me until the end,
and be my dear and truest friend.
This may be just a foolish dream,
but things aren't always what they seem.
Perhaps in time it will come true.
My loneliness may soon be through.
With a little faith in heaven above,
maybe soon I'll find the one I love.

RELATIONSHIPS

Beneath The Sea And Buried

Time has passed and things have changed more than I can expound.
There have been a lot of blessings in the changes I have found.
I've met a thousand people, and they've helped me all the way.
I've grown much closer to the Lord with every passing day.
I've made a million mistakes, but they did not bring me down.
I rose above and conquered them, to stand on solid ground.
Though faced with tragedy and pain as forceful as the tide,
the Savior never quit on me, He stayed there by my side.
And now I look back on this ever devastated path,
Once shaken with confusion and destroyed with furious wrath.
Now looking back the wounds have healed, and I am much more strong,
But there's one thing that has not changed and still feels very wrong.
My life has metamorphosed and everything is new.
The only thing that hasn't changed is I am not with you.
It's strange the way our lives take shape and only move apart,
when they were meant to be together from the very start.
Though mountains stand between us, and they seem too steep to climb,
the feelings that I have for you, have held their course through time.
There are rocks beneath the sea that do not move or wash away,
though beneath the sea and buried they still have the will to stay.
Time will drift away forever quickly turning to the past,
but my love for you unnoticed to eternity will last.

REPENTANCE

Take The Garbage Out

In a loss, one faces sorrow.
It's a risk you always take.
When the consequences follow,
there are choices you must make.
You can tabulate the damage
and repair what fell apart.
Or you can be the victim of
depression of the heart.
But you know that when you're wounded,
there are things that you must do.
When a snake bites you can't wait there,
hoping help will come to you.
It is painful when you falter.
It can make your life a wreck.
But in time you have to bounce back,
if you want to save your neck.
With a grasp on a new future
and awareness of the past,
you can rise above the wreckage
with a wisdom that will last.
When you're shattered by a problem,
and you don't know what to do;
there is always a solution,
and it all begins with you.
When the dust begins to settle
sweep it up and throw it out.
You'll find life is a lot better
when you take the garbage out.

REPENTANCE

Mending The Sails

On treacherous voyages of the sea,
vessels set out to prove their might.
The perils ahead are not easy to see,
for they face them in day and night.
The tides are unsteady and frequently shift
and can readily turn one astray;
but the stalwart vessels won't easily drift
and continue along on their way.
Still at times the wind roars with mighty howls,
and waves crash in from every side;
when the tormented ocean opens its bowels,
to destroy the great ship and its pride.
Submerging the vessel into depths below,
depriving it of any known course;
the evil sea laughs with its conquering blow,
without showing a sign of remorse.
The ship then floats up to the surface again,
full of water and terribly torn.
The once proud ship now only feels lowly pain,
and its weakness may bring it to scorn.
The fall of this vessel may seem quite a loss
and may cause it to drift as though dead;
but a true mighty ship can find hope through the dross
to recover and press on instead.
By patching the hull with the new and the secure,
throwing everything broken away;
and then mending the sails so that they can endure,
the once lame ship will be on its way.
Looking forward, determined to finish its trip,
the great craft moves swiftly to succeed.
For in moving ahead, it may frequently slip,
but enduring will bring greater speed.
It is not what's behind that will help one improve,
though we all need to live and progress,
It is picking yourself up and starting to move
ever forward that makes you your best.

RESPONSIBILITY

Nobody Owes You Anything

Stop, wake up, and look around.
Refrain from sobbing on the ground.
The debt of all to you is not,
it seems that you have missed the plot.
In youth, your parents paid your way
while you, unmindful, went to play.
Your path was marked with disregard.
Why do they say that life is hard?
The youthful mind arrayed with awe,
a prosperous life without a flaw.
It all would come so easily.
While sheltered it was plain to see.
Your destiny, you knew it all.
The world was at your beck and call.
For everything was owed to you,
and one day it would all come due.
The loyalty and wealth of all,
the souls of men both great and small
would serve your pleasure at your feet.
Your quest for status made complete.
But please wake up and look around.
There's not a servant to be found.
No Mom or Dad to pay your way.
No wealth at all to your dismay.
It all has been a wicked scheme,
a falsehood in some foolish dream.
You're not ahead, you're way behind!
In slumbering ease you have been blind.
Reality is hard to face.
The easy way has no more place.
Nobody owes you anything,
so stop pretending you're the king.
Successfulness depends on you,
your willingness to see it through.
Though money may not be your prize,
reality may make you wise,
if you don't turn the blame away
when tragedy has come your way.
The debts of all are yours alone,
and you must pay them on your own.
Wake up and see, you've left the nest.
It's time to lay the child to rest.

REVELATION

Ask The Lord

So you've come to the matter to see it resolved.
You have tried everything, but it still isn't solved.
You have looked at the problem from every side.
Everything you have learned, you believe you have tried.
But there still is one thing that you haven't tried yet.
The solution is there if you do not forget.
There is one final resource for sorting it out.
You should get on your knees, but you don't have to pout.
Ask the Lord for direction. He's waiting for you.
When you've done all you can, He will carry you through.
He expects you to do what you can on your own,
but when all else has failed, He won't leave you alone.
There is always a way, but sometimes we must ask.
Then the Lord will reveal how to conquer the task.
So don't ever give up. Anything can be done.
Just get down on your knees, and then call 9-1-1

SABBATH

Day Of Rest

It is crazy how everyone scurries about,
with no time to relax and no chance to get out.
On occasion, we all need to take a nice break,
for our bodily health and for sanity's sake.
When the Lord made the world, He had wisdom to see
that a day of reflection is necessary.
So He labored with diligence all through the week
He created the Heavens, the Earth, and the creek.
And He even made man in His image before
He sat down to relax on a beautiful shore.
With one day yet to come, when His work was complete,
He decided to take the next day off His feet.
And He saw it was good, with a smile and a nod,
so He took the whole day to pay tribute to God.
He created the Sabbath, a day to unwind,
that a Heavenly hope would remain in the mind.
On the Sabbath we focus with spirit and prayer,
and we're ready again for the mad world out there.
In the chaos of life, in a world so obsessed,
it is such a relief to have one day of rest.

SACRAMENT

As We Partake

Before we take the sacrament, we should review in mind.
Our every thought and action of the week we left behind.
To further dedicate ourselves to covenants we made.
To keep our spirits worthy and completely unafraid.
The Lord gave His own life for us. He bled from every pore.
He suffered for what we have done, our every sin He bore.
The sacrament is sacred, as it represents the Lord.
When taking it, our worthiness should never be ignored.
The symbols of His flesh and blood remind as we partake
that we must walk in righteousness with every step we take.
The sacrament renews our strength to carry on each day.
It keeps our footsteps certain, as we walk the narrow way.

SACRIFICE

Heavenly Treasures

As we follow the Savior, we turn from the Earth
to the Heavenly treasures of much greater worth.
We learn how to surrender what we may adore,
so in Heaven we find greater blessings in store.
As we keep the commandments and live by the plan,
are we doing the best that we possibly can?
We are proved and refined every day that we live.
A big part of our test is how much we will give.
Sacrifice is a lesson we all have to learn,
to give up something good for a better return.
Our dear Savior gave all that He had for our sake.
He cried out for our souls, though our sins made Him ache.
Then He hung on the cross where He suffered again
Thinking only of us, 'till His life reached its end.
Is it really so hard to give Him something back?
He should not have to suffer because of our lack.
There is nothing on Earth that we can't give away.
We should pay any price the Lord asks us to pay.

SALVATION

Rise Or Fall

There is nobody perfect. We all make mistakes.
There are times when we have some unfortunate breaks.
But this was no surprise. It was part of the plan
that our Father In Heaven created for man.
So He sent us a Savior to pay for our sin,
who could free us from all of the trouble we're in.
Only somebody perfect could carry our guilt
and endure all the pain and the blood to be spilt.
For each sin we commit leaves a permanent stain
that is only removed by enduring real pain.
So the Savior atoned for our foolish "mistakes."
But we're not off the hook, He decides who He takes.
If we do not repent and abandon the act,
then the Lord may take our sins and give them all back.
In our guilt we can not make it through Heaven's gate,
for the burden of sin holds us down with its weight.
But the Lord gave salvation, a free gift to all.
We will all live again, whether we rise or fall.
We will be resurrected and judged for our past,
and we'll need the Lord's help, or we'll face sentence fast.
For the Lord to assist us and free us from sin,
we must not say we're sorry, then do it again.

SELF-ESTEEM

Don't Stay Down

Take good care of yourself!
No, not just in your health.
Take good care of your feelings too.
If you want to achieve,
then you have to believe
there is something that you can do.
If your confidence fails
and depression prevails,
then you've already lost the war.
But you are not dead meat,
so get up on your feet,
and go get what you came here for.
Just how far you will go
and how much you will grow
are entirely up to you.
So if something goes wrong,
don't stay down very long,
never wait 'till the count is through.
Get back into the fight
and stand up for the right,
for you know you can win the bout.
If you treat yourself well,
you'll know after the bell
you will win by a big knock out!

SELFISHNESS

Resentful Words

Resentful words that strike the heart
destroy the mighty chains of love.
Two wounded souls that drift apart,
lose sight of all they once dreamed of.
Misunderstood. Feeling denied.
Contention only hears the worst.
And what was dear is thrown aside,
abandoned, left to die, and cursed.
A morbid path. A sullen grave.
A place to bury years of life.
A broken stone, too weak to save,
that once read happy man and wife.

SERVICE

The Savior's Errand

I am looking for a reason.
I need purpose to go forth.
I am looking for a challenge,
for a cause of greater worth.
Every man-made aspiration
has an end not far away.
I need something I can work for
and believe in every day.
I can not watch life go by me
like a storm across the sky.
I am not part of the landscape,
just to sit as time goes by.
There's a deeper, truer calling
we are all here to fulfill.
A purpose no one ever finds
when they are simply standing still.
We are watched by God in heaven.
Is that so hard to believe?
The proof in bounty lies abound
in endless blessings we receive.
Every day brings a new errand,
if we're willing to reach out.
As we grow closer to the Lord,
he shows us what it's all about.
So I am looking for a cause,
and every day there's something new.
For everybody who is willing,
there is service there to do.
All we need is to take notice
and help out each time we can.
We are on the Savior's errand
when we serve our fellow man.

SIN

Sin Is Like A Poison

There is nothing more disgusting, or appealing, than a sin.
There is nothing so offensive to be found dabbling in.
Still, however foul a sin may be, we all sin just the same.
So why do we still mess up then? Do we not have any shame?
A sin can hurt your credit faster than a credit card.
When people know you've sinned, sometimes they make life pretty hard.
Your name is turned to mud and everybody points at you.
Which makes no sense at all, since they have likely done it too.
What makes a thing so ugly, such a tempting thing to try?
When you give in to Satan, you can only wonder why.
He makes a sin attractive with a fancy wrap and bow.
But what there is inside the wrap, he does not let you know.
He builds your curiosity to have a closer look.
And then he pulls you in and you are swinging on his hook.
A sin is like a poison in a glass prepared to drink.
It shows us that it's wiser not to act before we think.

SPIRITUALITY

A Sudden Reminder

At the times when I'm down and I'm losing my grip,
when I feel like I'm sinking along with the ship,
there's a sudden reminder, a knock on the head.
And I come back to life, as though woke from the dead.
What a fool I have been in the daily routine.
It has darkened my way and demolished the scene.
What I lost in the world was my spiritual sight,
so I'm blind as a bat until I seek the light.
When I focus again with a heavenly view,
I gain spiritual strength that will carry me through.
When I'm down, I know I have forgotten the Lord.
That is one thing in life I can never afford.
If I don't like the feeling of being alone,
I should not call the Savior and hang up the phone.

STRESS

All I Want From Life

Look ahead! Watch your back!
Live for now. Stay on track.
What is life? All of this.
On your mark, don't you miss.
Everything, all the time.
Move ahead. Always climb.
Get a job. Break your back.
Save some cash in a sack.
Find a wife. Have a kid.
Got a house? Wish you did!
Go to school. Who needs sleep?
Don't you stop. You're in deep!
Car broke down. Better run.
Don't be late. You're not done.
What a joke. What a lie!
I've been had. How could I
fall for this? It's a scam.
Now I'm stuck in a jam.
Paycheck comes. Pass it on.
Nothing left. It's all gone.
Pressure's on. Doesn't stop.
I am sure I will drop
if I don't take a break.
What a pain. What an ache!
I complain. No one cares.
I hope God hears my prayers.
'Cause I hate how I live.
What I'd do. What I'd give
if I could have a day
now and then, just to play
with my kid and my wife.
That's all I want from life.

STRESS

Uncompleted Business

The room is filled with darkness, lying in the dead of night.
As I drift into unconsciousness, my outlook fills with light.
The uncompleted business of the day continues on,
and matters of concern unfold before me 'till they're gone.
Where what in life I cannot do, here nothing holds me back.
It doesn't make much sense, but in the end I'm right on track.
It seems so clear, while I am there, how worries are resolved.
But then when I wake up, I find that nothing has been solved.
My dreams escape my mind before my feet can hit the ground.
The answers from my slumber are all lost and can't be found.
I do my most impressive work while I am in my sleep.
But the rewards of my labor, I am not able to keep.
If I could just recall the work I did all through the night,
life would be so much more easy, everything would be just right.

STRESS

Plant A Seed

Why do you worry of time to come?
Have you dug yourself in too deep?
Why has your life grown so troublesome?
Has the climb become far too steep?
What has become of the carefree mind
that was once only filled with cheer?
Where are the words that were once so kind?
Has some fate made them disappear?
How has your view become so obscured
that you cannot see any good?
Why has your mind become so assured
that things wouldn't go right if they could?
Life is not over until you die,
and you still have so far to go.
Don't rush through life just to say good bye.
Give yourself room to live and grow.
Thought of the future is wise indeed.
It is helpful to plan ahead.
But sometimes it is better to plant a seed
and make peace with yourself instead.
Live in the present, the here and now.
Leave the future where it should be.
You'll feel at ease and you'll see just how
much more happy your life can be.

SUCCESS

The Hunt For Success

I have you now within my sight,
though you escaped me in the night.
I've learned your crafty, crooked ways.
The lifestyle that your kind portrays,
in seeking out the wealth to run
the business life. So where's the fun?
I've seen the struggle to succeed,
with those in power, full of greed.
And dead end options, what to do?
The big boys want to finish you,
but you alluded them quite well.
I tried to follow, but I fell.
And I went under, left for dead.
But over time I raised my head
and saved myself from sinking sand.
Now I am able to withstand
the crushing blows of those on top
and adverse pressure that won't stop.
Though there were times I was afraid,
I followed every move you made.
I learned your lessons, every one.
That to succeed, you have to run
and be aware of what's ahead.
Don't ever stop, press on instead.
Believe in everything you do
and while you're at it, have fun too.
I have you now within my sight.
This time I'm going to do it right.
With all I've learned, one thing is true.
I do best what I like to do.

TALENT

Talents Are Blessings

God has given us talents to use and explore.
That we may make of small things a little bit more.
God has given us talents to make life more fun.
He expects us to use them and get something done,
but the world makes a talent, a hard thing to find.
With the pressure of living one can feel confined.
In a labor where talent is hardly required,
it can be a great task to keep feeling inspired.
But our talents are blessings we cannot forget.
For a talent unused, turns into a regret.
What are we going to say when the Lord comes to see
what we've made of our talents and turned out to be?
Will we say that we settled for easier ways?
That we buried our talents and wasted our days?
Make the most of your talents, that's what they are for.
Never settle for less, there is so much in store.
When you use the great talents the Lord gave to you,
you will be a success in whatever you do.

TEACHING

Patience To Teach

I don't know any man more prepared for a trial,
than a man who is taught with a comforting smile.
It is stunning to see what a person can do
when he's taught to distinguish what's false from what's true.
It is hard to do well when you're eager to learn,
but no one has the patience to teach in return.
We all started as children who wanted to know,
asking, "what, why, and how," everywhere we would go.
And how wounded we felt when we heard someone say,
"I am busy right now, will you please go away?"
What a blow to a mind reaching out for advice!
Just a five second answer would surely suffice.
We are children of God, reaching out for the truth.
And we still need to learn, as we did in our youth.
We are never too old to be taught something new.
When we teach one another, we learn something too.
How much greater we are when we're willing to share.
Are we really too busy to show that we care?
To teach others may not seem important to do,
but it will when the one with the question is you.

TESTIMONY

No Greater Blessing

I was born in the fullness.
I was raised in the light.
With a firmness of duty
and knowledge of right.
As a child I was careful.
I did just what I should.
I obeyed the commandments,
for I knew they were good.
As I grew I was challenged.
Righteousness was despised.
My straight course was distracted,
while the truth was disguised.
There were times I was certain
that the spirit was there.
But sometimes I was blinded
and I just didn't care.
I have found this a cycle
that is hard to escape.
But with time it gets better,
as my life takes its shape.
I have a testimony
that the gospel is real.
And I know as I live it
the great joy that I feel.
There is no greater blessing
than to do what is right.
And as long as I'm living,
I will not quit the fight.

TRIALS

Lamentations Of The Traveler

Why hast thou led me here, my Lord?
What duty lies before me?
The money's gone, I can't afford
to live my life so blindly.
I left my home and people who
cared if I lived or died.
And here I am alone again,
left drowning in my pride.
In my prayers I asked for guidance,
and the answers made me sure.
Yet I set out on thy errand
and now I feel insecure.
I have followed thy direction,
persevered, and carried through.
Still my footsteps travel backward,
and I don't know what to do.
I cannot succeed on my own,
with my erring human hands.
I need thy ever loving care
to free me from these bands.
Please abide with me and lead me
in a course that's clear and true,
I've lost the strength to carry on
in this journey without you.
With thy support, I'll rise with strength
and I know I'll find success.
I will know where I am going
and no longer have to guess.

TRIALS

Our "Challenges"

The Lord has blessed mankind with love and beauty here on earth.
He gave us opportunity to grow and prove our worth.
For us he made the oceans and the mountains standing tall.
He offers answers to our prayers, to help us through it all.
Our Savior eased the way for us, with hope for our success.
He even suffered for our sins that we might suffer less.
For these things we are thankful. They uplift and make us strong.
But we are not so thankful when the paths we take are wrong.
Sometimes along the journey obstacles stand in our way;
our challenge is to overcome without going astray.
This challenge grows more difficult when we achieve a goal,
defeating one great problem, just to fall into a hole.
Soon we can see that trials are not ever going to end,
and tasks become more difficult the further we ascend.
But challenges are building blocks that we can use to climb.
They shape a simple soul into an edifice sublime.
The Lord gave us adversity to make our weakness strong.
In life we gain endurance on the path as we press on.
Our "challenges" are also *gifts* deserving much respect,
for they are all rewards that the Lord gives to His elect.

TRIALS

Who Is Perfect?

I do not know how wrong I am,
but I am often told.
How easily they point at me
when I don't fit the mold.
I don't do what the others do
at times it's not for me.
But others like to tell me how
I really ought to be.
So many like to take control
and tell you what to do.
They claim to know most everything,
but they don't have a clue.
What might be someone's treasure chest
is someone else's pit.
What gives one man incentive,
makes another want to quit.
If there's someone who is perfect,
please stand up and lead the way.
Otherwise please keep your silence,
'cause I don't have time to play.
Time is short to make a difference
and there's so much to achieve.
In the world there is so little
that one can truly believe.
Do the best with what your given,
trust the Lord to lead the way.
Though the world may be uncertain,
He will not lead you astray.

TRUST

Into The Air

Long ago I climbed a ladder to a roof of twenty feet,
thinking nothing of the matter, or the fate that I would meet.
There was work that must be done and as the light one, I should go.
But as I worked upon the roof, I faced a danger down below.
I was left there all alone while I was working on the top.
There was no one there to steady me, or help me should I drop.
Still I thought I'd be just fine, I'd done it many times before.
And I never thought that this time I'd come crashing to the floor.
But the feet of that great ladder weren't as firm as they should be,
and before I knew it that ladder slipped out from under me.
In a horror I fell down onto the concrete like the rain.
My arm shattered into pieces, and I shuddered from the pain.
I have never been the same since then. I've become scared of height.
Now each time I see a ladder, it is not a pretty sight.
But when I fixed our roof at home, I'm so glad that you were there.
You held the ladder firmly, and you took the time to care.
Still I was scared to come back down, I had a second thought.
A fear of height I'd never known, froze me right on the spot.
I walked around a little bit and knowing you were there,
I overcame my fear, placing my feet into the air.
I reached the ground safely this time, because I was with you.
Your love helps me do everything I don't think I can do.

VALUES

It Matters To Him

You are judged by your values, by what you esteem,
and by how hard you've worked when you've run out of steam.
You define who you are by the time that you spend,
and the way you can stick with a task to the end.
Every measure of worth and importance to you,
can be plainly apparent in all that you do.
You may not feel it matters what others may think.
They can all think the worst and you won't even blink.
But your values do matter to someone who sees,
and it may not be wise to do just as you please.
For the Lord is aware of your thoughts and your deeds.
He knows all of your wants. He knows all of your needs.
And it matters to Him what you feel is of worth.
That is why He allowed you to come to the Earth.
The Lord knows who you are and how much you can do.
He wants your full potential to come shining through.
So hold on to your values and don't let them go,
or the Savior will be the first one who will know.

WICKEDNESS

Follow Through

As the past has made clear,
man begins to lose fear
of engaging in wickedness.
In complacency's ease,
mankind seldom foresees
the result of their foolishness.
As the miracles fade
and the Lord's hand is stayed,
man begins to lose moral ground.
Every sin once abhorred
with the conscience ignored,
becomes commonplace all around.
Then the Lord will step in,
wielding justice for sin,
when the wicked are more than good.
In a miracle's path
with the Lord's mighty wrath,
once again man does what he should.
But man can't get away,
he will still have to pay
for the foolishness he will try.
Why does man turn his back
when he's given some slack?
Why does wickedness take God's place.
Why can't we follow through,
in the best of times too,
with the gospel that we embrace?
Can't we learn from the past
and move forward at last?
Why take roads that we know are wrong?
When we're on the right track
we should never turn back
with the Lord is where we belong.

WISDOM

Climbing High

I don't claim to be perfect.
There is much I don't know.
But I'm gaining on wisdom,
though my learning is slow.
My mistakes are not numbered.
I lost count of them all,
but I learn my best lessons
after each painful fall.
There is much to be learned
on a challenging climb.
With persistent hard work,
wisdom will come in time.
So I'll keep falling down,
but I'll keep climbing high.
If I reach for the stars,
I'll at least reach the sky.
I'm a long way from perfect.
That is not hard to see.
But I'm sure a lot wiser
than I used to be.

WORK

My Part

Is it true that God will help me if I only help myself?
They say if you want things done right, then you should do them yourself.
How does my faith fit into the plan when everything is through?
If I've done all of the work myself, what's left for God to do?
Does God only intervene when I can carry on no more?
Or when life is much too difficult to make it through a chore?
Is great faith alone enough to get the miracles I need?
I have had a lot more faith in life than just a mustard seed.
Still I have not seen a mountain move, not even one small stone,
'til I've given it my best and made an effort of my own.
I imagine how I'd feel if all the work was done for me.
What a waste of time my life would be if everything was free.
If there were not any purpose, what on Earth could I live for?
If I didn't work for something, life would really be a bore.
I cannot expect the Lord to give me blessings while I sit.
I can wish upon a star, but that will not help me a bit.
Yes it's true, that God will help me after I have done my part.
But I can't expect a thing, until I've tried with all my heart.

Index

Topics	Page	Titles
Achievement	1	When I'm Gone
Aging	2	More Than We See
Appearance	3	Don't Take Me As I Am
Atonement	4	Thoughtless Deeds
Attitude	5	All Under Control
	6	Your Own Way
Baptism	7	The First Leap
Blessings	8	Recognizing Blessings
Charity	9	How To Give
Children	10	Just A Kid
Choices	11	Lessons Of Life
Christ, Jesus	12	Tears In The Rain
	13	That Man Upon The Wall
Christmas	14	The True Meaning Of Christmas
	15	A Legend Of Santa
Commandments	16	Why We Have Commandments
Commitment	17	Set Into Stone
Communication	18	Who Will Listen?
Compassion	19	Childlike Eyes
Conscience	20	Hear The Voice
Contentment	21	It's Time For Resolutions
	22	The Spending Game
Courage	23	Learn To Jump
Dating	24	The Right One
Death	25	I Will
Determination	26	Why Do Want?
	27	I'll Be Free, Or I'll Die
	28	To The Top
Discipline	29	Take The Blame
Endurance	30	Get On Your Feet
Faith	31	Grown From A Seed
Family	32	Is It So Wrong?
Fatherhood	33	Something You Should Know
	34	The Most Joyous Gift Of All
	35	The Busy Man Behind The Scene
Focus	36	"Heartwork"
	37	Plain And Simple
	38	Just For You
Forgiveness	39	More Than You Will Ever Know
Free Agency	40	Choosing The Right
Friendship	41	A Friend
Goals	42	A Goal
	43	Are You Happy Where You Are?
God	44	If Only
Gratitude	45	The Work That You Do
	46	What I Really Want To Say
Happiness	47	They Might Have Joy
	48	You Need Some Fun
Heaven	49	Purpose In Heaven
Holidays	50	The More Happy Side Of Life (Thanksgiving)
	51	The Alarm Was To Blame (Labor Day)
	52	The New Year Will Be Better (New Year's Day)

Topics	Page	Titles
	53	When The Easter Bunny Comes (Easter)
Honesty	54	If Everyone Were Honest
Humor	55	People Who Frown
Humility	56	Treasures Of The Road
Integrity	57	I Am Not Afraid
Jealousy	58	The Envy Of Man
Kindness	59	To Lift Each Other
	60	Kindness
Knowledge	61	What You Don't Know
Leadership	62	A Good Leader
Life	63	Seasons
	64	What Is It That Matters
	65	That Great And Glorious Day
Love	66	I Have Everything
	67	Something To Enjoy
	68	You And I
	69	Out Of The Darkness
	70	All Along It Was True
	71	It Sure Must Be A Miracle
Marriage	72	Stronger With Age
	73	It's Perfect Now With You
	74	To Share Eternity
	75	My Eternal Friend
	76	Eternity With You
Missionary Work	77	Good News
Morality	78	Never Follow The Crowd
Motivation	79	Ability
Motherhood	80	The Best A Mom Can Be
	81	It's Great To Be Your Son
Obedience	82	One Great Test
Optimism	83	What Is Right
Parenthood	84	Easy To Say
	85	Beyond Any Compare
	86	Aint This The Life?
Patriotism	87	America
Peace	88	Like A Child
Prayer	89	It All Starts With A Prayer
Pre-Existence	90	Freedom Is Power
Pride	91	Is It Evil?
Procrastination	92	Time To Snooze
	93	Worst Things First
Profanity	94	Is Anyone Offended?
Progression	95	Deserving Of Praise
	96	The Climb
	98	A Mission To Fulfill
Prophets	99	A Truly Great Man
Relationships	100	Memories Never Made
	101	When I'm A Fool
	102	Something Like The Wind
	103	Foolish Cares
	104	A Foolish Dream
	105	Beneath The Sea And Buried
Repentance	106	Take The Garbage Out
	107	Mending The Sails
Responsibility	108	Nobody Owes You Anything

Topics	Page	Titles
Revelation	109	Ask The Lord
Sabbath	110	Day Of Rest
Sacrament	111	As We Partake
Sacrifice	112	Heavenly Treasures
Salvation	113	Rise Or Fall
Self-esteem	114	Don't Stay Down
Selfishness	115	Resentful Words
Service	116	The Savior's Errand
Sin	117	Sin Is Like A Poison
Spirituality	118	A Sudden Reminder
Stress	119	All I Want From Life
	120	Uncompleted Business
	121	Plant A Seed
Success	122	The Hunt For Success
Talent	123	Talents Are Blessings
Teaching	124	Patience To Teach
Testimony	125	No Greater Blessing
Trials	126	Lamentations Of The Traveler
	127	Our "Challenges"
	128	Who Is Perfect?
Trust	129	Into The Air
Values	130	It Matters To Him
Wickedness	131	Follow Through
Wisdom	132	Climbing High
Work	133	My Part